The Dambuster who Cracked the Dam

The Dambuster who Cracked the Dam

The Story of Melvin 'Dinghy' Young

Arthur G. Thorning

Pen & Sword
AVIATION

First published in Great Britain in 2008
and again in paperback format in 2013 by
PEN & SWORD AVIATION
An imprint of
Pen & Sword Books Ltd
47 Church Street
Barnsley,
South Yorkshire
S70 2AS

ISBN 978 1 78303 015 6

Printed and bound in England
by CPI Group (UK) Ltd,
Croydon, CR0 4YY

Pen & Sword Books Ltd incorporates the Imprints of Pen & Sword Aviation,
Pen & Sword Family History, Pen & Sword Maritime, Pen & Sword Military,
Pen & Sword Discovery, Pen & Sword Politics, Pen & Sword Archaeology,
Pen & Sword Atlas, Wharncliffe Local History, Wharncliffe True Crime,
Wharncliffe Transport, Pen & Sword Select, Pen & Sword Military Classics,
Leo Cooper, The Praetorian Press, Claymore Press, Remember When,
Seaforth Publishing and Frontline Publishing

For a complete list of Pen & Sword titles please contact
PEN & SWORD BOOKS LIMITED
47 Church Street, Barnsley, South Yorkshire, S70 2AS, England
E-mail: enquiries@pen-and-sword.co.uk
Website: www.pen-and-sword.co.uk

To Angela, Rebecca and Edward
without whose help this book could not have
been written

Contents

Contents

Acknowledgements

I must start by thanking Mrs Clare Hopkins, Archivist, Trinity College, Oxford who asked me to write a biographical note on Melvin Young for the 2003 College Report, thus starting my research and interest in his story. I must also thank Clare for her continuing support answering my numerous questions, and the recent former President of Trinity, Mr Michael Beloff QC and his secretary Mrs Yvonne Cavanagh.

I also wish to thank most sincerely Melvin's family who have been both encouraging and supportive, in particular: his sister Mrs Angela Sturr (Dr Angela Rowan Young MD), his brother-in-law Mr Edward Rawson and his niece by marriage, the late Rebecca Rawson, who generously provided invaluable material left by Melvin's wife Priscilla, the late Mr Dodd Young and his cousin and god-daughter Mrs Bridget Corby (nee Nendick).

Melvin's schools have been of enormous help in my research and I would like to thank especially: Mr Richardson W. Schell (Headmaster) and Mrs Kathy Nadire, Kent School, Connecticut; Mrs Pam McNeil, The Webb Schools, California; Mr Eddie Smith, Westminster School, London; Mr Nigel Taylor (Headmaster), Amesbury School, Hindhead, Surrey.

With regard to other important aspects of Melvin's life I would like to thank: Mr Peter Elliott, Royal Air Force Museum, Hendon; Mr Robert Owen, Official Historian, 617 Squadron Aircrew Association; Squadron Leader Dick Stanton and Mrs Chris Fretwell, Oxford University Air Squadron; Mr Jaap Kroon, Bergen Remembrance and Friendship Association; Mr Brian Riddle, Librarian, Royal Aeronautical Society; the staff of the RAF Air Historical Branch, the National Archives, the Imperial

War Museum, The Law Society, Hitchin Library and the British Library Newspaper Department.

Mr John Hawkins of Melvin's freemasonry lodge was very helpful with that aspect of the story.

I must also thank the following for help and information:

Mr Harry R. Humphries, Mr Tony Iveson, Mr Ted Wass, Mr John Jackson, Dr John Sweetman, Squadron Leader Ray Leach, Mr Geoffrey Sturr, the late Mr Alan Tyser, Mr Richard Rowland (Kingston RC), Mr Michael Jones (Leander), Mr David Young, Miss Kelly Russell (River and Rowing Museum), Mr David Mitchell, Mr Hugh Disney, Mr Thompson Webb, Mr Alex Bateman, Mr Geoffrey Allsebrook, Mr John Entwisle (Reuters), Mr Les Munro, Mr David Ross, Mr Scott Field (Parkinson Archives), Ms Hazel Simpson (BBC), Mrs Linda Jones, Mr Stephen Nendick, Air Chief Marshal Sir Thomas Prickett, Mr Scott Pottbecker (Marvelwood School, Connecticut), Mrs Elizabeth Boardman (Brasenose College, Oxford), Mr Andrew Mussell (Lincoln College, Oxford), Mr Ian Sayer, Mrs Lorna Read (Naval Historical Branch), Mrs Margaret Taube Harper, Mr Jonathan Falconer, Mr Fred Sutherland, Squadron Leader George Johnson, Mrs Barbara Pettey.

I am grateful to Crecy Publishing Ltd (www.crecy.co.uk) for permission to include extracts from *Wellington Wings*, by F. R. Chappell.

Finally, I thank my wife Valerie for her consistent help and support in the project of researching and writing this book.

Introduction

At 21.47 on 16 May 1943, Lancaster ED887/G, AJ-A of 617 Squadron, lifted from the grass at RAF Scampton piloted by Squadron Leader Henry Melvin Young, DFC and Bar, as part of Operation Chastise. At 00.43, on 17 May, Young flew low down the Möhne Lake in Germany on a heading of 330° magnetic towards the dam, levelled the 30 ton aircraft at 60 feet above the water at a speed of 220 mph and the 'Upkeep' depth charge was released. It made three good bounces, hit the dam wall, sank to 30 feet, exploded and the dam started to crack. At 02.58, having followed Guy Gibson to the Eder Dam as his second-in-command, Young and his crew were shot down and killed as they crossed the Dutch coast at Castricum-aan-Zee, north of Ijmuiden. Such was Melvin Young's historic, heroic and tragic last night.

Operation Chastise, the raid on the Ruhr Dams on the night of 16/17 May 1943, was an epic of courage, determination and ingenuity. The physical effect on Germany's war effort was serious, although less than strategic planners had hoped. However, the moral, political and psychological impact, at a time when victory was unsure and distant, was great. Churchill, in Washington at the time, was able to point to this remarkable feat of arms as a signal success.

Melvin Young's life, leading up to this most famous operation, was notable enough, without this tragic climax. Of Anglo-American parentage, he was educated at several schools on both sides of the Atlantic, before attending Trinity College, Oxford where he achieved a good degree in Law and rowed in the Boat

Race against Cambridge. He learned to fly with the Oxford University Air Squadron and, following the outbreak of the Second World War, became a bomber pilot. He had numerous adventures, surviving two ditchings in the sea (thus his nickname 'Dinghy') and was twice awarded the Distinguished Flying Cross, for operations over Germany, Italy, Malta and the Western Desert. In 1942 a posting took him to the USA where he married Priscilla Rawson, whom he had known since he was at school in America.

Chapter 1

Family Background

Henry Melvin Young, known as Melvin, was born on 20 May 1915 at 11A Lower Grosvenor Place, Belgravia, London. His father, Henry George Melvin Young, was recorded on the birth certificate as a Second Lieutenant, 4th battalion, Queen's Royal West Surrey Regiment (a solicitor). His mother was Fannie Forrester Young, formerly Rowan, an American from a socially prominent Los Angeles family.

Lower Grosvenor Place is an imposing row of buildings in the 'French Empire' style, on the Grosvenor Estate, facing the wall of Buckingham Palace garden – very much at the heart of the British Empire as it then was. Thus Melvin was, like Winston Churchill, the son of an Anglo-American union; his story reflects this balance of the traditions of the Old World with the energy of the New.

Melvin's father, Henry George Melvin Young, known to family and friends as Harry, was born in December 1876, the son of Walter William Young, who had a successful solicitors' practice in London. Walter's father, William, had married Mary Ann Melvin, a Scot, at the fashionable church, St George, Hanover Square, London, in June 1839. Melvin was subsequently used as a name by the family.

Walter Young was born in 1840, and his sister, Amelia Melvin, in 1847, both at Marylebone. Sadly, their father William died in 1847 and the 1851 census shows Mary Ann Young as the head of the household, aged 40, with her occupation as a draper. By 1861 the family was in Southwark and both Mary and Walter, now 20, were described as haberdashers. In December 1866, Walter married Mary Ann Hannah Packham at Chelsea and together they had seven children, of whom Melvin's father was the fifth.

By 1871 Walter was a solicitor's managing clerk, his career in the law was developing and the family had moved to Battersea, where they employed a young servant, Jane Taylor, who notably had been born at Bengeo, Hertfordshire. Walter's career prospered and he founded his own solicitors practice. The family moved progressively to another house in the Battersea area of London and then to the cleaner air of Bengeo, on a hill just above the county town of Hertford, some twenty miles north of London. Walter died aged 80, on 4 October 1920, suffering a heart attack at Kings Cross station in London, while running to catch a train to Hertford after a successful day's work at the office.

Henry had an older brother Walter, who suffered from epilepsy as a child but overcame this to qualify as a solicitor. Sadly he died at a relatively early age, whereas Henry died in 1963 aged 86. Henry had two older sisters, May Mary and Helen Amelia, who were sent to Germany to further their education, and a younger sister Florence Emily. He had two other brothers; Francis, known as Tommy, who went to Cambridge followed by St Bartholomew's Hospital where he qualified in medicine, and Charles, who farmed in South Africa. Their mother died at the age of 39 (29 April 1883) and Henry had little recollection of her and was sent to boarding school at an early age along with Francis and Charles. In 1885, Walter married Sarah Ann Parsons at St George, Hanover Square – Sarah, who was twelve years younger than Walter, came from Folkestone in Kent

The family seems to have kept its connections with Battersea, but had a house at Bengeo where the summers were spent and where Henry's parents, along with his stepmother Sarah, are buried in Holy Trinity churchyard. Henry was educated at Berkhamsted School along with two of his three brothers, before moving on to Trinity College, Oxford in 1895. At Oxford Henry was a keen oarsman and represented Trinity at Henley, winning the Thames Cup in 1898. Unfortunately for Henry, Trinity did not quite make Head of the River at Oxford in his time (2nd in 1896, 3rd in 1897 and 4th in 1898). He graduated in 1898 with a

Third Class Honours degree in Law, and joined the Honourable Society of Gray's Inn, where he was called to the Bar in 1900.

In 1906 Henry set out with his friend Cyril Bretherton, later a respected editor and poet, to the United States of America. They sailed to New Orleans, intending to go to San Francisco to practise law. They had introductions to law firms and were on their way when the great San Francisco earthquake occurred and so instead went to the then smaller city of Los Angeles. Both Henry and Cyril Bretherton were admitted to the California State Bar without any difficulty. Henry practised law in California until 1913, but he had plans to return to England, since he had qualified as a solicitor and is listed by the Law Society of England and Wales as being admitted to the Roll of Solicitors in November 1911, working for his father's firm, W. W. Young, Son and Ward, who had offices in London.

Melvin's mother, Fannie Forrester Rowan, was born in 1883 to George Doddridge Rowan and Fannie F. Rowan (née Arnold). She had six brothers and a sister, Florence. Fannie's parents had moved from Chicago, where their first son Robert Arnold Rowan was born, to California in the 1870s to benefit from the warm climate. Robert A. Rowan became a leading real estate developer in Los Angeles; indeed there is still a Rowan Building, at 460 S. Spring, built in 1911 in the Beaux Arts style by the renowned architect John Parkinson, who designed Los Angeles City Hall. Parkinson also designed the Alexandria Hotel for Rowan and another developer, across the junction from the Rowan building; this was Los Angeles' social centre for two decades and hosted a glittering clientele from the Southern California film industry, national figures and foreign royalty (including Edward, Prince of Wales). The family fortunes were subsequently closely linked to the success of R. A. Rowan & Co.

Fannie Rowan attended the Marlborough School for Girls in Los Angeles. On graduation she hoped to join some of her friends at College at Stanford or Berkeley, but these institutions were thought by her parents to be unsuitable for young ladies – too much drinking, dancing and card playing – so instead she attended a finishing school in Washington DC, the Mount Vernon Seminary. Thereafter she travelled with her mother, sister and one of her brothers to Europe for some two years, living with a French family and visiting Germany and Italy. She returned to Los Angeles in 1907 where she was noted as a tennis player in the Southern California Championships. At this time she met Henry Young and, after a long engagement, they were married in 1913 and moved to London, where Melvin and his sisters, Mary and Angela, were born.

Chapter 2

Childhood

Shortly after their marriage in 1913, Henry and Fannie Young moved from California to London, where Henry worked with his father and brother in the family law firm, W. W. Young, Son and Ward, who had offices at 24 Ely Place, Holborn Circus, EC1 and 251 Lavender Hill, SW11. However the peace of Europe and, eventually the world, was shattered in 1914 and Henry found himself in the British Army until 1919. He was serving as a Second Lieutenant in the Queen's Royal West Surrey Regiment at the time of Melvin's birth. Henry became a Captain, was Assistant Inspector of Quarter Master General Services and was mentioned in dispatches in August 1918. One of the earliest photographs of Melvin, aged about 3 and dressed in a sailor suit, is a studio portrait with Henry in the uniform of a Captain.

Although Fannie was well travelled, it must have been quite an upheaval for her to exchange the sunny skies of Southern California for the often grey ones of London, and the more rigid society of pre-1914 England, closely followed by the uncertainties and privations of war which coincided with her pregnancy with Melvin. Melvin was a large baby, weighing in at over nine pounds; indeed he was to grow to be 6 feet and 1 inch tall. Fannie had a hard and tiring delivery and recuperated in the apartment overlooking the walls of the Buckingham Palace garden.

Also living with the family at the time was Jane Green who was 'the house parlour maid that came with the flat'[1] Jane's fiancé had died in the early days of the First World War and she accepted the position of nanny to the family for the next twenty-five years, moving back and forth to America with them. Angela recalled that 'Melvin, Punkie (Mary) and I were devoted to her (Jane) and I think my Mother was jealous to a certain extent'.

Two years later, in 1917, Melvin's sister, Mary Arnold Young, was born at the house in Wimbledon to which the family had moved and where they lived until 1919 when Henry was demobilized at the end of the war. Mary, always known by her nickname of Punkie, was a remarkable person. After a sickly start in life, due to coeliac disease (gluten intolerance), she eventually was well enough to attend Wycombe Abbey School and thereafter the nursing school at St Bartholomew's Hospital. She worked in London as a nurse during the Blitz and then studied midwifery at the Radcliffe Infirmary in Oxford. At the end of 1943 she went to Africa on missionary work. Returning in 1947, she entered Trinity College, Dublin and qualified in medicine and converted to Roman Catholicism. She then went to India where she met Mother Teresa and was the first doctor with the Missionaries of Charity in Calcutta. Tragically, she died in 1961, after an operation which could not save her life.

After the First World War the family continued to live in London, but made two trips to the USA, when Fannie's mother died, to visit relatives and also to consult doctors about Mary's medical condition. There are photographs of Melvin in a palm-lined road in California, with his mother and Mary on the beach on Santa Catalina Island and with his Aunt Florence, possibly at the Biltmore Hotel in Santa Barbara. After visiting doctors on both coasts of the USA and in Europe, Mary was finally diagnosed, by Sir Frederick Still at Great Ormond Street Hospital for Children, as having coeliac disease. There was some doubt about whether Mary would survive, but her health began to improve by trial with diet and after a period at a sanatorium in Switzerland.

During this period, in 1924, with the family now living in Kensington, at Cresswell Gardens, another sister, Angela Rowan Young, was born. Two years later when Melvin was at his preparatory school, Amesbury, Fannie took Angela, Melvin and Mary to Switzerland for some months, for Mary's benefit. There are photographs of Melvin with Angela when she was a small child in London. Angela also went to Wycombe Abbey

School and eventually qualified in medicine firstly in England, at the London School of Medicine for Women, and subsequently in the USA. Angela remembers Melvin as '...a wonderful big brother – he persuaded my father and mother to let me go to medical school at a critical time'. Melvin would also drive to Wycombe Abbey School from Oxford and take Angela out in his car - strictly against the school rules.

In 1955 Angela married George Sturr, a teacher, and they had seven children. Angela combined raising this large family with a busy career as a gynaecologist, practising as Angela R Young MD, in California, where she now lives in retirement.

Throughout his youth Melvin enjoyed horse riding and the first photographs of him on horseback are at the age of six, both in a park and on Eastbourne Sands. He is also pictured wearing 'Aunt Ethel's' riding hat and boots and accompanied by her dog. 'Aunt Ethel', Mrs Reginald Martin, and her sister, Miss Alberta Wake Gearing – 'Aunt Bert'- were friends of the family, residing at Tunbridge Wells. Indeed Alberta was Melvin's godmother and took a great interest in him throughout his life; she kept a room for him at her London apartment as he grew up and, notably, it is recorded as his address in his RAF Record of Service. As a teenager, when he was at Westminster School, we find Melvin riding with Aunt Ethel – Ethel was an accomplished horsewoman and rode to hounds, side-saddle. At the age of twelve there are photographs of Melvin with a friend sailing their model boats on the Round Pond in Kensington Gardens, a short walk from Victoria Road, where the family now lived, and Aunt Bert's apartment in Kensington Court Gardens, that area of red brick mansion blocks now much favoured by foreign embassies. The Young family also had a beach hut at Littlehampton.

Melvin seems to have been an active and healthy child, although he was very susceptible to rashes from contact with poison ivy, which caused his face to swell. (He had an unwelcome brush with this plant during his honeymoon in California!). He was also rather flat-footed and was not happy with sports that involved running – thus his inclination towards riding and rowing. He was naturally left handed, albeit the educational fashion of the time made him learn to write with his right hand. His handwriting was rather awkward and it is notable that he preferred to use a typewriter later in life. But he did manage to sign his name with a flourish and he had a lifelong habit of sitting cross legged, often on the floor or on a desk.

Notes
1. Private correspondence with Angela Sturr.

Chapter 3

Schooldays

Melvin Young attended four schools before going up to Trinity College Oxford. It is notable that all four schools are still in existence and thriving – the quality of education which they provided served him well. The schools were, in order of attendance:

Amesbury School, Hindhead, Surrey, England
Webb School, Claremont, California, USA
Kent School, Connecticut, USA
Westminster School, London, England.

Amesbury School was founded in 1870 and moved to its present site in Hindhead in 1917. The main building was designed as a school by the foremost architect of the time, Sir Edwin Lutyens and, as such, is unique, Lutyens being more famous for country houses, memorials – including the Cenotaph in Whitehall – and Imperial buildings in Delhi. There is a photograph of Melvin in school uniform outside this building. In the 1920s the headmaster was Mr C.L. MacDonald (known as Clem to all his pupils) and it seems he was an acquaintance of Melvin's father. Mr MacDonald was a popular and well-respected teacher who provided a comprehensive education and was supported by a handpicked staff. He would read stirring stories to the smaller boys in his study and, on Saturdays, would show black and white films and invite lecturers to give illustrated talks.

Melvin was at Amesbury until 1928 when, with his mother and sisters, he moved to the USA; his father followed some six months later having wound up his business interests in London.

The Amesburian (the school magazine) recorded at the end of that year that H.M. Young would 'continue' in America – his school contemporaries moving on to such well known British schools as Haileybury and Charterhouse. Had the family stayed in England, Melvin would have gone to Charterhouse. According to his mother he had just failed to get a scholarship to that school but had been accepted and was to have been placed in the same class as the scholars. However, 'family circumstances' necessitated their moving to California.[1]

The magazine also records that Melvin was a member of the school shooting team, being one of the best marksmen, he did some boxing and was a member of the Foxes scout group. Melvin was one of five pupils to be awarded a Star Prize in his final year – an academic prize but not one of the school's two key prizes. It is interesting to record that in May 1928 a party of twenty-nine senior boys visited Portsmouth at the invitation of Captain Lambert of the aircraft carrier HMS *Courageous*. After first visiting HMS *Victory* they had 'a sumptuous tea' on *Courageous* and were given guided tours of the ship – it is likely that Melvin was one of these boys and this experience may have helped to trigger his interest in aviation. It is sad to record that HMS *Courageous* was sunk by a German U-boat in September 1939.

In 1922 Thompson and Vivian Webb leased what was then the abandoned home of the failed Claremont Boys School, just above Claremont, California, and started the Webb School – continuing to this day as The Webb Schools; The Webb School of California and the Vivian Webb School. The grandson of Thompson Webb, Thompson Webb III, has collected the recollections of his grandfather and combined with material provided by the school it is possible to reconstruct Melvin's time at this school.

Having moved to Los Angeles in the summer of 1928, Fannie Young enrolled Melvin at the Webb School in September. He stayed until June 1930, when at the age of fifteen he became the youngest boy to graduate from that school. Thompson Webb recorded that he was 'amazed at a boy so young being so well advanced' and 'took his hat off' to the English school which

Melvin had previously attended.

The Webb School archives tell us that as well as his 'remarkable scholastic record' he liked sports. In particular he favoured riding and was an enthusiastic member of the gymkhana team. In those days many Webb boys kept horses. It seems that Melvin's Uncle Dodd, who had riding horses at his ranch at Cielito Lindo in Hidden Valley, provided him with a mount. There is a photograph of Melvin, annotated 'California age 14', showing him on a horse in typical Californian surroundings (probably at Webb School). The outdoor nature of Californian life is reflected in the fact that the summer term at Webb was based at Camp Robin Hood, Lake Arrowhead. Also, in the summer of 1929, Melvin was sent half way across the continent to the Culver Naval School for a two-month summer camp, which (according to Fannie) he enjoyed immensely and which gave him much physical exercise. The Culver Camps started in 1901 and continue to this day in the best American tradition of summer camps for youths. At that time Melvin had yet to put on his 'growth spurt', being 5ft 4in tall and weighing 108lbs.[2] Melvin is commemorated at The Webb Schools to this day – on the War Memorial in the Vivian Webb Chapel and as a 1930 graduate on the door of the Jackson Library. Melvin's nephew, Geoffrey Sturr, attended The Webb School in the 1970s and spoke with two faculty members who knew and taught Melvin, Dr Thompson Webb and Dr Raymond Alf; they remembered him fondly.

It does seem that this was a period of severe tension in the Young family; Henry and Fannie disagreed about the education of their children and Fannie wanted to increase the family by adoption. Eventually Fannie took two boys under her wing, Robert and Dodd. Dodd was indeed adopted and his family carry on the Young name in California. Thompson Webb records that Fannie Young came to him during Melvin's first year at the school and asked him to find a place, secretly, in another school, as she feared that Henry would take Melvin back to a school in England. Thompson and Vivian Webb took Melvin and his trunk to the Catalina Island School where he remained for a few weeks. However, thereafter, Melvin returned to Webb and stayed for two years until he graduated from the school in 1930.

Whatever the level of family dissention, Henry stayed in the Los Angeles area until 1933 when he and the children returned to England without Fannie. Henry, now in his fifties, had found it difficult to resume his legal career in California two decades on. The tension in the family had been such that at one point Fannie accused Henry of trying to kidnap the children. However, Angela states that Melvin, Mary and she joined their father in England of their own free will.

Henry resumed his career as a solicitor in Hertford – this location was partly for reasons of familiarity (his parents had lived nearby) but mainly because when he sold his previous business interests he had undertaken not to practise within twenty miles of central London. His new premises were at 117 Fore St, Hertford and for a time he rented a house at New Road, Broxbourne, where Angela lived with him and their family nanny, Jane Green, until she was old enough to follow Mary as a boarder at Wycombe Abbey School. Later Henry moved to a flat in the same building as his office in Hertford.

It is notable that Henry's great interest in rowing had continued, because he helped the British Rowing team during the 1932 Los Angeles Olympic Games, and the Youngs entertained many of the competitors at their Spanish style house, situated in two acres of land on the exclusive Palos Verdes Estates, overlooking Santa Monica Bay. Melvin was in Los Angeles for this event (in the summer vacation after leaving Kent School) and his interest in rowing, developed at Kent School, can only have been encouraged. It is an interesting sidenote that this house was damaged by a landslip caused by the 'Long Beach Earthquake' of 10 March 1933 which measured 6.1 on the Richter scale. Henry had just stepped inside the living room after standing on the lawn to watch the sunset (about 6 p.m.) when the earthquake occurred – much of the garden disappeared leaving the house on the edge of the cliff, and the family had to move to Fannie's mother's cottage in nearby Redondo Beach. A lawsuit ensued over the composition of the cliff!

When Melvin graduated from Webb School his parents thought he was too young to move to the nearby Pomona College, and Melvin himself wanted to follow in his father's footsteps and prepare for entry to Oxford University. He may also have been encouraged in this ambition by the fact that his cousin, Bob Rowan, had spent two years at Merton College, Oxford, while Melvin was at Webb School. Bob Rowan studied economics and philosophy at Oxford, but his studies were interrupted by the need to return to Los Angeles to look after the family business, which prospered under his guidance – he also became a collector of modern art, and the Rowan Collection is to be found at the Mills College Art Museum in Oakland, California.

Kent School, Connecticut, had been recommended to Fannie Young as being a good next move for Melvin and she engaged in a long correspondence with the headmaster there. Kent School was at first reluctant to take a boy into the senior forms. One of the teachers at Webb School was Paul Squibb, himself an alumnus of Kent and, at Fannie's request, he supported Melvin's case by writing to Kent saying that Melvin was 'a splendid student and an adaptable one' and that 'without giving up his English ways and manners he has managed to fit into this lot of Californians very well'.[3]

By July 1929, Melvin had achieved creditable grades in College Board examinations in English (73 per cent), Latin (70 per cent), Maths (77 per cent) and French(63 per cent); there were plans for him to take further subjects in 1930. The headmaster of Kent School advised Paul Squibb that he felt he would be able to 'make a very good course for him next year' and confirmed this with Fannie Young.[4] Thus Melvin crossed the American continent and started at one of the best boarding schools, Kent School, located in north-west Connecticut, between the Appalachian Trail and the Housatonic River, some ninety miles from New York City. The school sits in beautiful, hilly, wooded country on the side of the Housatonic, with the town of Kent just across the river. It has many fine buildings, some of which were there in Melvin's time, including the stone built chapel.

The school was founded in 1906 by the Reverend Frederick

Herbert Sill, a member of the Order of the Holy Cross (OHC) which is a Benedictine Anglican monastic community founded in 1884 by James Otis Sargent Huntington to provide a specifically North American expression of monasticism; today the order comprises five houses in the USA, Canada and South Africa. Frederick Sill had graduated from Columbia University in 1894 at the age of twenty and four years later was ordained and began his ministry in the Church. He retired as active headmaster in 1941 but remained as Headmaster Emeritus until his death in 1952 aged seventy-eight. He was known to his students and their parents as 'Pater'. Father Sill founded Kent with a vision which is captured in the school motto: Simplicity of Life, Directness of Purpose and Self-Reliance. He was also committed to educating students 'from all walks of life' and so there was a 'sliding scale tuition' in which families paid fees which he felt they could afford – this policy remains, in principle, at Kent School.

Father Sill played a leading role in founding the English Speaking Union Student Exchange Scheme in 1927 and many British boys spent time at Kent as a consequence. As a student Frederick Sill had spent several vacations in England, exploring the country by foot and bicycle, sometimes with friends and sometimes alone. He travelled the whole length of Hadrian's Wall by bicycle and once, in Somerset, he stopped to look at a parish church and, finding that the incumbent was also called Sill, called at the vicarage to meet his namesake. All his life he used to surprise his English friends by the extent of his knowledge of their country. Soon after the First World War, in 1921, he was again in England and he began to think how he could form some permanent link between Britain and his school at Kent, and the Exchange Scheme owes much to his initiative. Father Sill was a keen rowing coach, having been coxswain in the Columbia University boat, and thus Kent was very much a rowing school. During this 1921 trip, he visited Henley-on-Thames and, looking along the regatta course from the bridge, decided that Kent crews would someday take part in the regatta – they did on numerous occasions from the late 1920s, winning the Thames Cup in 1933 and have had one of the most distinguished school records in the regatta over the decades.

Melvin was at Kent School from 1930 to 1932. He is recorded as being 'a great favourite and he always thought of himself as a Kent boy' – indeed he was to be married in the school chapel and in 1942 addressed the students about his war experiences. While at Kent 'he participated in Hockey, Crew [i.e. rowing] and Chess Club' (his sister Angela remembers him as a keen chess player). Although Melvin was not an exchange student, he would have been pleased to be joined by an English boy, Thomas Ingram, for the year 1931-32 under the Exchange Scheme. Thomas Ingram recalled (writing in 1960):

> It can easily be understood that Pater's influence on those English boys who have been lucky enough to know him has been great. Yet he never tried to impress his personality upon us. His intention from the start was simple: it was to strengthen the bonds between his country and ours. He once said to me 'When you think of America, don't think of democracy and our common heritage, but about the homes where you have sat at the fireside and been happy'. He was never pedantic and never, as far as I can remember, gave the impression that he was trying to teach me anything. He often had delightful surprises. My diary records one such:
>
> 5th November 1931. Today has been a very good day. The Old Man came up to me and said 'It's Guy Fawkes day, isn't it?' So I thought round for a bit and then – brightly – 'Oh yes, so it is. Could we have some fireworks, Sir?'
>
> 'No but you can have a holiday.'
>
> So, in Assembly he said 'All English boys stand up' I began to think there might be something in it. And sure enough it was...a whole holiday!
>
> The question was, what to do? Melvin Young and I went for a huge long walk all morning. We had a marvellous tramp: out past the field house and along the river: then up and over to Hopkins Lake. Here we stopped quite a long time by the little boat house. The sun was warm but there was a marvellous sting in the air. Nearly all the leaves are now down and line the bottom of the lake. All around the trees are very gaunt. In the middle of the lake there was a

spring which keeps the water very clear. It looked lovely with the most perfect saddlebacks behind. We skirted the left of the lake and came back by Macedonia. We followed the creek down about a mile,   jumping from rock to rock…We came out by the ranch and walked back along the road.

A day of formal education would hardly have left such an impression. Here was a New England Fall making its unforgettable mark upon an English boy; and Pater knew very well that it would if only the two could be brought together.

One of Melvin's classmates was Edward (Ed) Rawson whose family had a house nearby, Ravenscroft Farm on Skiff Mountain, a few miles, and a long climb, from Kent School. It stands on a green plateau surrounded by forest and hills. Melvin often went to dinner there and sometimes stayed with them in the vacations – it was a long way to California. Ed's mother, Clementine, was impressed by Melvin because 'he was so polite and intelligent'.[5]

The Rawson family traces its ancestry back to another Edward Rawson (1615-1693), who was the Secretary of the Colony of Massachusetts from 1650 to 1683. About the time of the Civil War, one of the Rawsons started a successful pork-packing business in Cincinnati and this provided a solid base for the family's fortunes. Edward's father, Hobart Rawson was the Chief Engineer of the Long Island Railroad. The men in the Rawson family have a long tradition of attending Harvard University, although Ed also attended Yale Law School; many of the women in the family went to Bryn Mawr College, near Philadelphia.

Melvin came to regard the Rawson household at Ravenscroft Farm as a home from home, in a situation of normal family life. And it was Ed's elder sister, Priscilla, who was destined to become Melvin's wife. Priscilla, who was a graduate of Brearley School New York and Bryn Mawr College, studied music in England just before the Second World War and their relationship developed at that time.

The Kent School 'Old Main Building' is also a former farmhouse. When 'Old Main' was renovated after the war,

Melvin's mother-in-law, Clementine Rawson, dedicated the 'Melvin Young Room' in his memory; there is a plaque in the room and a picture of Melvin above the fireplace – the plaque reads:

THIS ROOM IS IN LOVING MEMORY OF HENRY MELVIN YOUNG
A KENT BOY. CLASS OF 1932.
1915-1943

Every new student at Kent School is welcomed to the school in the Melvin Young Room, which is now part of the admissions office. Melvin is also commemorated on the war memorial in the school chapel. Melvin clearly developed a strong attachment to Kent; in his will, written a week before his death, he made a bequest of fifty pounds to the school.

When Melvin left Kent he received a handwritten graduation certificate from Reverend Sill, dated 9 June 1932, which reads:

To Henry Melvin Young -
To certify that he is a Graduate of Kent School of the Class of 1932 and is awarded a diploma.
May our dear Lord bless and keep you. I shall miss you. You have been loyal and faithful. I hope that you will come back soon.
Your loving pater
Frederick H Sill OHC
Headmaster of Kent School

There is no evidence that Melvin had very strong religious feelings but he was undoubtedly influenced by Father Sill and the Anglo-Catholic ethos of Kent School – perhaps, like many young men, Christianity sat lightly on his shoulder and he was content to follow the routine observances. His RAF Record of Service shows him as 'Church of England', and – as we shall see later – he came under the influence of the Anglo-Catholic 'High Church' Oxford Movement at the beginning of the war. He was not musical but did enjoy church liturgy and Angela recalls a day, early in the war, when she, Mary and Melvin attended High Mass at the Brompton Oratory in London; Mary eventually

became a Roman Catholic nun. Melvin became godfather to
Bridget Nendick, the daughter of his cousin Kathleen.

In 1931-2, there was a young exchange teacher at Kent, Arthur
Harrington Franklin, known as 'Bill', from Westminster School.
Bill Franklin, born in London in 1903, the son of a civil servant,
had been educated at Merchant Taylor's School, London and
went up to Lincoln College, Oxford in 1922, where he was a
classics scholar. He was President of the Junior Common Room
at Lincoln College and gained a rowing Blue. Indeed, he gained
the distinction as the only Blue never to have rowed the full
course of the Boat Race. He was the spare man in the Oxford
VIII in 1925, joined the crew when one member fell sick after the
last training course had taken place and then, due to the
appalling weather conditions in which the race took place, the
Oxford boat sank! He was an Assistant Master at Westminster
School from 1926 to 1939 and although called to the Bar at the
Inner Temple in 1931 he did not practise as a barrister, becoming
instead an ordained priest in 1935. He became friends with
Melvin and accompanied him on what must have been an
adventurous drive across the USA to California, when they both
left Kent in 1932. Ed Rawson recalls the story of this drive,
recounted later, as involving several mishaps en route, not least
due to 'having too much treacle in the radiator'. Both Melvin
and Bill Franklin are pictured with Priscilla Rawson in
Connecticut in June 1932, beside a convertible roadster with
running boards of which any gangster would have been proud.[6]

As a clergyman, Bill Franklin served as a padre in the army
during the war, including a period in the Middle East, and was
mentioned in dispatches. He kept in touch with Melvin's sister,
Mary, and eventually proposed marriage – but Mary was determined to pursue her medical studies and declined; in 1948 Bill
married the Hon. Joan Pond and had two daughters and two
step-daughters. Bill Franklin served for many years as Rector of
Great Leighs in Essex, and also as Rural Dean of the Rodings
and as an assistant master at King Edward VI School,
Chelmsford. He was appointed MBE and awarded the
Territorial Decoration for services to the Reserve Forces. He had
a great influence on Melvin, and, no doubt, on many others.

During his period at Kent School, Fannie Young had been in correspondence with Father Sill about the future of Melvin's education. There was clearly a plan that Melvin should follow his father, Henry, to Oxford University, albeit the route there was uncertain. Fannie Young was keen to ensure that Melvin did not get 'completely out of sympathy with American ideals' and wanted him to 'feel he belongs to both countries'. Should he go to an American University first and then, as a Rhodes Scholar, to Oxford?[7]

This was a time when the education of the Young children was causing a rift between Fannie and Henry. The immediate solution for Melvin after Kent was to enrol him at Pomona College at Claremont, California, not far from Webb School. Melvin's file at Pomona, where he stayed until early 1933, is sparse but indicates that he was interested in languages and in becoming a lawyer. Writing to Father Sill, Melvin admitted that 'Pomona did not work, for me, for many ways, doubtless much my own fault. They were chiefly interested in scientific education.' Henry believed that Pomona was only a stop-gap and that Westminster School in London would provide a suitable preparation for Oxford.

Thus, in April 1933, Melvin left California for England. Mary, accompanied by their nanny Jane Green, went later by train to Montreal, then by ship down the St Lawrence River and across the Atlantic, in time to start at Wycombe Abbey School. Henry left with Angela from San Pedro, near Long Beach, on a cargo ship which sailed through the Panama Canal arriving at Tilbury, on the River Thames, near London, after a journey taking a month.

On his way to England, via New York, Melvin was able to make a brief visit to Kent School. Writing to Father Sill from the RMS *Majestic* a few days later[8] Melvin said:

I shall be writing to you soon from Westminster and telling you about that. I expect I shall find everything very strange after five years away, but England or New England I shall always like. Now just a line to tell you how much I enjoyed my visit to Kent even for those few hours. You cannot imagine the pleasure it gave me to see the school just for the day even....So Sunday at School was a return and a new start in a different direction – only this time East is the right direction I am sure.

Father Sill had provided Melvin with a final recommendation, dated 19 April 1933:

To Whom it may concern: This is to certify that H. Melvin Young graduated from Kent School in June 1932 with honours. He received a certificate of honourable dismissal and was admitted without further examination to Pomona College, California. He has an unusually good mind and an agreeable personality. I have no hesitation in recommending him.

All this change and uncertainty in Melvin's life was occurring against a background of world financial upheaval. After the Wall Street crash of 1929 times were hard. On board the *Majestic* Melvin noted that there were many people who were concerned about the rate of exchange and the British coming off the Gold Standard. Passengers were saving their dollars until they got to England to change them. The ship was 'pitifully empty'; about 100 tourist passengers and 150 in first class, whereas the total capacity was over 2,000. The White Star Line was to collapse the following year and be incorporated into its main rival Cunard. The *Majestic* was the largest liner on the Atlantic at the time, being replaced by the *Queen Mary* a few years later. Melvin commented that they were having very fine weather, which was 'very lucky for a bad sailor like myself' – it must have added to the pleasure of the experience. He ended his letter to Father Sill saying that he looked forward to seeing him and rowers from Kent School at Henley that summer – when they were destined to win the Thames Cup.

Westminster is an ancient school. Its origins can be traced to 1179, when the Benedictine monks of Westminster Abbey were required by Pope Alexander III to provide a small charity school. Its continuous existence is certain from the early fourteenth century. After the dissolution of the monasteries in 1540,

Henry VIII personally ensured the school's survival by statute, and his daughter, Elizabeth I, confirmed the royal patronage in 1560, with a new charter for 'The College', and is celebrated as the School's Foundress.

The Westminster School magazine is titled *The Elizabethan*. It carried a brief obituary for Melvin which records that 'He was placed in the Sixth and quickly made his mark by his personality and his ability, both at work and on the water'. It also records that he gained his Pinks (school colours for rowing) and that he 'went up to Oxford and distinguished himself as an oar'. Other school records show Melvin rowing at number 3 in a school competition in Junior-Senior Fours in October 1933; notably his weight, 11st 8lbs, was the heaviest in the whole competition. He is recorded as winning the Junior-Senior Sculls, beating Humphreys by two and a quarter lengths in 4 minutes 27 seconds, having won his heats 'easily' and by four lengths.

The Westminster boat house is on the Thames at Putney, the starting point of the annual Oxford v. Cambridge Boat Race – perhaps this location inspired him with a desire to row for Oxford. Melvin's RAF service record shows that he was a corporal in the Westminster School Officers Training Corps from 1933 to 1934. As in the case of Kent, he remembered Westminster in his will, leaving fifty pounds to the School Society. Melvin Young is recorded, along with many other Westminster alumni who died in war service, on the organ case in the main hall, known as 'School', and in an illuminated War Memorial Book.

Notes
1. Letter from Fannie Young to Father Sill re. Melvin's academic prowess, 13 April 1929.
2. 7 stone, 10 lbs, application form to Kent School, 10 May 1929.
3. Letter from Paul Squibb to Father Sill, 20 May 1929.
4. Letters from Father Sill to Paul Squibb, 19 February 1930, and Fannie Young, 30 April 1930.
5. Ed Rawson's words.
6. Ed Rawson thinks it was a Buick.
7. Letter from Fannie Young to Father Sill, 23 March 1931.
8. Letter from H.M. Young to Father Sill, 22 April 1933.

Chapter 4

Oxford – Law, Rowing and Flying

So, in 1934, Melvin followed his father and went up to Trinity College, Oxford, to study law. Trinity College was founded by Sir Thomas Pope in 1555. A devout catholic with no surviving children, Thomas Pope saw the foundation of an Oxford college as a means of ensuring that he and his family would always be remembered in the prayers of its members. He came from a family of small landowners in Oxfordshire, trained as a lawyer and rose rapidly to prominence under Henry VIII. As Treasurer of the Court of Augmentations he handled the estates of the monasteries dissolved at the Reformation, and amassed a considerable personal fortune. Pope was a discreet and trusted privy counsellor of Mary Tudor, and it was from Mary and Philip that he received Letters Patent and royal approval for his new foundation. Pope died in 1559. Although his religious ideals were never fully realized – Elizabeth had succeeded her sister in 1558 and England returned to the Protestant faith – nonetheless the memory of his name, like his college, has endured the fluctuating fortunes of some 450 years.

Thomas Pope purchased the site and buildings in Oxford of an earlier monastic foundation, Durham College which, from 1286 until the Reformation, provided a place of study in Oxford for a small number of monks from the Benedictine Cathedral Church at Durham. Its buildings comprised a single quadrangle which provided hall, chapel, library and rooms. The only surviving Durham College building is Trinity's Old Library, which was completed in 1421. The name Trinity is thought to echo the original dedication of Durham College: to the Trinity, the Virgin and St Cuthbert. In the succeeding centuries, many new buildings have been added – some designed by Wren including one of Oxford's finest chapels – and extensive gardens. The front quadrangle is particularly attractive with lawns and trees; its boundary with Broad Street partly comprises a row of seventeenth century private houses, known in the college as The Cottages.

It was a room in these cottages which became Melvin's initial accommodation at Trinity. In his second year he lived in a set of two rooms above the Chapel Arch, now part of the Senior Common Room, with one of the best views in Oxford, over Trinity's leafy front quadrangle and over the historic Durham Quadrangle to the rear. He shared these rooms with Paul Cooke, the son of a bank manager, who had come to Trinity in January 1935 from St Edward's School, Oxford, to study law. Paul Cooke was a good rugby player and was awarded Blues in that sport (i.e. played against Cambridge) in both 1936 and 1937. He also played for England. He achieved a third class degree in 1937 but sadly was to die in the Second World War. The use of this fine pair of rooms may well have been a tribute to sporting success. In his third and fourth years at Oxford Melvin moved out of college, as was normal, and lived at 8 Oriel Street, just off the High.[1]

The college which Melvin entered in 1934 was basically unchanged, in buildings and ethos, from that to which his father, Henry, came up in 1895. Most of the undergraduates were from professional and land-owning families and were confident of their place in the upper reaches of British society. They were largely drawn from well-known British public schools; independent foundations, many of considerable antiquity. Melvin had such an education, but with the extra advantage of having attended two excellent schools in the USA as well. There was a strong athletic tradition at Trinity which was at its peak in the 1930s. In 1938, for instance, Trinity won the Rugby and Athletics Cups, as well as becoming Head of the River. This tradition had been fostered by members of the college's governing body, and in particular by the Law Tutor, Philip Landon who was on the governing bodies of several schools, including St Edward's from which he recruited Paul

Cooke, Melvin's sometime room mate, to boost the rugby team. Landon also took a personal interest in the development of the Trinity College Boat Club by encouraging applications from likely candidates.

By modern standards the academic principles of the college might have been considered relaxed, albeit with many notable exceptions. Philip Landon has been quoted as saying that if his students '...could not get a first they should try to get a Blue!' Melvin wrote to Father Sill, from his godmother's home in London, a month before he went up to Oxford[2] relating that he had received a letter from his prospective tutor 'giving me a list of books to read this summer, with exams on the second day up'. He confirmed that his family now planned to live in England (no mention of his mother) and that he expected to go into the law 'though whether to the Bar or as a solicitor is not certain, probably the latter as I don't think my powers run to advocacy'. However, as an additional preparation for a career in the law, Melvin was admitted as a student of the Honourable Society of Gray's Inn, in April 1935, although he was never to be called to the Bar. His referees were Bernard Campion of Gray's Inn, and a solicitor, Thomas Arnold Kirkham, a long time friend of the Young family.

Given his disinterest, indeed lack of ability, in sports which involved running, it is not surprising that Melvin took a major part in rowing, firstly for the college and ultimately for the university against the arch rival, Cambridge. His time at Kent School and Westminster School had served to develop this ability. His earlier love of horse riding, encouraged by Uncle Dodd's horse at the Webb School in California, found an outlet in the cavalry section of the Oxford University Officers Training Corps (OTC). Indeed, in 1936 the OTC was called upon to provide some of the mounted troops lining the streets of Windsor as the funeral cortège of King George V made its way from Windsor Station to the Castle. Melvin was one of the mounted men on that sombre winter day, made more doleful by the tolling of the Sebastopol Bell at the Castle.

One of Melvin's friends and contemporaries at both Westminster and Oxford was J.C.H. Cherry, who went up to

Brasenose College. Conrad Cherry was a remarkable young man and his friendship with Melvin was strong. In 1940 he married Glory Rowe, whose brother rowed with him in the victorious Oxford crew of 1937, and they had a daughter, Susan, born in 1942. It has been said that the revival of Oxford rowing which had been in the doldrums for a decade – Cambridge had won every race from 1924 to 1936 – was due more to Cherry, both as an oarsman and as President of the Oxford University Boat Club (OUBC), than any other man. He rowed for Oxford against Cambridge in 1936, 37 and 38 – in 1938 as President of the OUBC, in the winning boat with Melvin rowing at No. 2. The Times reported that 'Cherry's style is the most perfect of any post-war heavyweight oarsman'. He represented Great Britain in the XI Olympiad at Berlin in 1936, rowing in the eights – sadly they came fourth, behind USA, Italy and Germany, so he only acquired the 'participant's medal'. Conrad Cherry was Leander Club Captain in 1938 and 39. He was described by the Principal of Brasenose, Dr Stallybrass, as:

> ...not easy to know intimately... and liked none but such as he believed to be very honest men. Water was his element. At Westminster, at Oxford, yachting in the holidays and during the war he spent his life on the water.

When the war came Conrad Cherry took a commission in the Royal Naval Volunteer Reserve (RNVR). His commanding officer wrote:

> Con was easy to talk with and make friends with for he was so simple in all his faiths and had such a kind philosophy. Before he had been with us three months I would not have willingly exchanged him for any [regular] RN officer.

He thus seems to have been the sort of quiet, honest personality to have appealed to Melvin, and no doubt vice versa. He served in the minelayer, HMS *Welshman* which, because of its high speed (40 knots), was used for hazardous missions carrying vital stores to and from Malta; indeed the role of the ship was featured in the film *The Malta Story*. HMS *Welshman* was torpedoed and sunk off Tobruk by *U-619* on 1 February 1943, with heavy loss of life, including Lieutenant Conrad Cherry.

It is clear that for Melvin, apart from his law studies which he worked at hard enough to get a good, second class honours degree, rowing was his main interest during his time at Oxford. Among his successes as an oarsman were wins in the OUBC Coxswainless Fours in 1936, the Pairs and Sculls in 1937 – in which year he also rowed in the Isis crew – the Oxford second boat – and in the Oxford boat against Cambridge in 1938. The 1936 Coxswainless Fours deserve a mention, since it was actually a dead heat with Oriel College. Notably the Trinity team was coached by Con Cherry and included Frank Waldron, who also rowed in the 1938 Oxford boat. Melvin's oar from this event, suitably decorated with names and the Trinity crest, resides, along with his Boat Race oar, at the home of a relative in California to this day.

As well as rowing at Oxford, Melvin also represented Trinity, and occasionally the Leander Club, at the Henley Royal Regatta over several years. Although he never won an event, he rowed in many: Ladies Plate 1935; Visitors and Goblets 1936; Ladies, Visitors and Goblets 1937; Grand and Stewards 1938. He was a keen member, along with his father, of Leander and the Kingston Rowing Club, on whose war memorial he is commemorated. Indeed his father, Henry, was a committee member of the Kingston Rowing Club and took a house there one summer. Henry's friend Thomas Kirkham was chairman of that club and was also one of Melvin's referees for his application to Gray's Inn.

Such was Melvin's enthusiasm for rowing that he left notes for the Trinity College Boat Club (TCBC) on the rigging of boats and sizing of oars for crews of different weights and, ultimately, in his will he left his rowing books and some rowing equipment to the college, as well as £20 for the purchase of silver tankards. One of his major ambitions was that Trinity should return to its position as Head of the River at Oxford, last achieved in 1864. This ambition was achieved in 1938 and the position was held until 1949, albeit with some interruption during the war. Melvin's notes record that the 1938 boat was rigged with a slide of 17 inches and a leverage of 31 inches, with

12 foot oars, of which 3 feet 8½ inches were inboard. The Trinity boat made five 'bumps' (in four races), overcoming Oriel, Brasenose (no doubt to Con Cherry's chagrin), Magdalen, Balliol (Trinity's neighbouring college and traditional rival), and New College.

Once again, writing to Father Sill about their mutual passion of rowing,[3] Melvin recounted that:

> Our Eights Week ended last Wednesday, and the College has barely recovered from the Bump Supper we had that night, as we made five bumps and went to the Head of the River for the first time since 1864. We had a very heavy crew averaging 12st. 11½lbs (179½lbs if my arithmetic is right) which is exceptional for a College and within a pound of our last Varsity boat which was one of the heaviest ever.

He explained that their coach had been 'Peter Haig-Thomas the great Cambridge coach', although for the forthcoming Henley races they would be coached by 'Tom Brocklebank, the Cambridge stroke from 1928-30'. Melvin ended his letter expressing a desire to get together with the crew from Kent School which was coming to Henley and that he 'could have the pleasure of showing them Oxford and giving them lunch or tea'.

This successful Trinity crew included two notable characters, Frank Waldron and Richard Hillary. Waldron should have rowed in the 1936 Olympic Games, but was taken ill with chicken pox at the wrong moment. Hillary went on to posthumous fame due to his book *The Last Enemy* which recounted his exploits in the Battle of Britain and as one of Sir Archibald McIndoe's plastic surgery burns 'guinea pigs'. Hillary's story is well documented elsewhere, but it is notable that of the eight oarsmen in that boat, only two survived the Second World War, and Waldron, serving in the Scots Guards, only after a serious head injury.

Four of the eight died serving in the RAF; the other two were Flying Officer Alwyn Stevens who was the second pilot of a 99 Squadron Wellington bomber which came down in the sea only 150 yards from the shore at Felixstowe on 7 November 1940 and Flight Lieutenant Derek Graham who was killed in an accident flying a 247 Squadron Hurricane fighter on 24 October 1941. The last two who lost their lives were John 'Sammy' Stockton, a captain in the Scots Guards, who was killed in the final drive to Tunis at the end of the North Africa campaign on 27 April 1943, and Captain Richard Furlong of the Royal Artillery, who died in the Rhineland Campaign on 21 March 1945.

Having graduated in 1937 (Jurisprudence, including Roman Law, Contract, Torts, Legal History and Law of Land), Melvin continued his 'studies' at Trinity and concentrated his efforts on getting a Blue, rowing against Cambridge. He did however, succeed in entering the Oxford University Air Squadron, to satisfy his latent interest in flying, but it seems that when pressed he gave his time to rowing. The competition to get a place in the Oxford boat was (and no doubt remains) intense. The Oxford versus Cambridge Boat Race is still a national institution, but in the 1930s was more prominent as a sporting event and received heavy newspaper coverage. One newspaper reported of Melvin:

> Was thought to be unlucky last year, for he was one of the best blades in a very good Isis crew. Was passed over this year again, and several men were tried before Young was called upon and given preference. Got in largely because two earlier choices strained their backs, but would have been extremely unlucky if he had been omitted. Just the kind of racing oarsman Oxford have been looking for. Follows two other oarsmen from Westminster who have gained high honours – M.P. Lonnon, last year's Cambridge President, and J.C. Cherry the present Oxford President.

In his modest way, Melvin was later to address the boys at his old school, Kent:

> I had always been a clumsy oarsman, both at Kent and Oxford, and my instructors found me clumsy flying. So I was detailed to fly a bomber. Flying a bomber is not unlike being the middle man in an eight-oared shell.

The Times, on Boat Race Day, 2 April 1938, stated:

Young at No. 2 is a little short and slow [presumably referring to his rowing style] by reason of his stiffness, yet he has won many races against quicker, more supple oarsmen by sheer hard work.

The weeks leading up to the Boat Race were necessarily hectic with preparation and training. Again these preparations were covered in some detail by the newspapers, especially *The Times*. The Oxford crew were coached initially by H.V. Page, formerly Captain of the Thames Rowing Club, for some five weeks in the middle of their preparation by Dr Mallam, and for nearly a month at the end by Mr G.O. Nickalls, a distinguished member of the Leander Club. Oxford, who had decided to use the winning 1937 boat, went out twice on the Friday a week before the race, not returning until it was almost dark. The crew then spent the weekend at Goring Heath and returned to the tideway on the Monday (28 March) rowing, by themselves, in disturbed water with a continuous swell. A couple of days later they had their last serious work on the tideway before the race, this time in company with the Cambridge 'Goldie' crew. The day before the race, Friday 1 April, the Oxford crew had two outings on the Thames; firstly at 1 p.m. when they practised starts followed by a short row at 5 p.m.

The Oxford crew for the 1938 Boat Race was:

1. J.L. Garton	Eton and Magdalen	11st 10lb
2. H.M. Young	Westminster and Trinity	13st 0lb
3. R.R. Stewart*	Eton and Magdalen	12st 13lb
4. H.A.W Forbes	St Paul's and Magdalen	13st 1lb
5. J.P. Burrough*	St Edward's and St Edmund Hall	13st 7lb
6. F.A.L. Waldron	Shrewsbury and Trinity	13st 10lb
7. J.C. Cherry*	Westminster and Brasenose	13st 12lb

8. A.B. Hodgson*   Eton and Oriel   12st 0lb

Cox. G.J.P. Merifield King Edward VI, Southampton
                     and St Edmund Hall   7st 13lb
* Indicates Old Blue

The Oxford crew were some half a stone heavier on average than their Cambridge opponents, and this was to be beneficial in the rough conditions encountered during the race. There was a strong wind from the west-north-west and this caused the tide to be late, so the start of the race was delayed from the scheduled 1.45 p.m. until 2 p.m. This, the ninetieth University Boat Race, was given a live broadcast on BBC radio, by three commentators, John Snagge, Tom Brocklebank and Edgar Tomlin, from the launch *Magician*. Cambridge won the toss and chose the Surrey station. There was rough water from the start and it turned out to be one of the best races for years. For three quarters of the race the crews were overlapping, but eventually Oxford gained a clear lead and, despite a determined effort by Cambridge, they held on to win by two lengths in a time of 20 minutes and 20 seconds.

Melvin's sister, Angela, and his father, Henry, were able to experience the excitement of the event, especially Oxford's winning surge, from a launch following the race. Henry had persuaded Wycombe Abbey School to let Angela have leave for the occasion and he drove out and took her to London, although the school insisted that she should return as soon as the race was over; schools were sterner then! Hospitals were also very disciplined, and Mary had to remain at her duties at St Bartholomew's. Angela wrote to her mother in California to tell her all about it.

The finish of the race was one of the first occasions when the fledgling BBC television service attempted an outside broadcast. The BBC had a camera near the finish and viewers (restricted by transmission limitations to parts of London at that time) were able to see both boats 'quite plainly until they were hidden from view by the willows on the river bank'. From a position in the enclosure, the crews were seen bringing in their oars and boats after the race – apparently the public were very interested by the novelty of the TV cameras. That evening the Oxford crew celebrated at a dinner, presided over by Con Cherry, at the United University Club.

In 1937 Melvin was accepted, after an unsuccessful application in 1935, into the Oxford University Air Squadron (OUAS). On his application to the OUAS he gave his sports and interests as rowing, motoring, riding (OTC Cavalry) and aeronautics. The college recommended him as being 'strong, healthy and energetic'. The OUAS selection committee (chaired by Dr Stallybrass of Brasenose College) gave him a mark of alpha and he was accepted on 15 October 1937. The next day he attended a medical examination by Dr F.G. Hobson of 20 St Giles and was passed as 'Fit for flying up to Air Force Standard'. Melvin then commenced learning to fly on the Avro Tutor biplane at RAF Abingdon. There are letters on Melvin's OUAS file from which it is clear that he worked hard at combining his flying training with his rowing, albeit his ambition to get a Blue was paramount. In particular he asked for as much 'pre-term' flying as possible immediately after the Boat Race.

By the end of the 1938 Annual Attachment (summer flying camp) he had flown some forty hours. This flying camp was held in July at Ford Aerodrome, near Littlehampton on the south coast of England, familiar to Melvin and his family from their beach holidays. His instructor, Flight Lieutenant Charles Whitworth, who was to be station commander at Scampton at the time of the Dambuster raid, noted:

This member is not a natural pilot and is still rather coarse on the controls. He improved considerably during the fortnight. He is very keen and has plenty of common sense. He made some good cross country flights.

(Author's note: Which of us, who are pilots, have not had a comment about being coarse on the controls at some point?)

Melvin's final note to the OUAS, on 25 July 1938, thanks the Chief Flying Instructor, Wing Commander F.L.B. Hebbert, for receipt of his log book and 'A' licence – the equivalent of a modern Private Pilots' Licence – and his OUAS Proficiency Certificate.'

There were many members of the OUAS who later achieved fame. The debonair Richard Hillary and Frank Waldron from Trinity were in the Squadron; but Waldron soon found that he suffered from airsickness and eventually distinguished himself in the Scots Guards. As might be expected, there were many Oxford sporting 'stars' in the OUAS; Prince Obolensky, the international rugby player, famous for a winning try against the All Blacks, was one of these. It would have been hard to imagine a more attractive 'flying club' for a young man in the 1930s – in modern times the University Air Squadrons continue to give valuable service, but more definitely as part of the RAF Training process.

Perhaps the most notable of this 'Golden Generation of the Air Squadron' was a law student from Merton College – Geoffrey Leonard Cheshire. Leonard Cheshire – like Melvin he was known by his second name to avoid confusion with his father – was to become the most distinguished of bomber pilots, winning the VC, the DSO and two Bars, the DFC and completing 100 bombing missions. In 1943, he was promoted, becoming the youngest group captain in the RAF, aged twenty-five but in October that year, at his own request, dropped a rank to take command of 617 Squadron. In 1945 he was offered his 101st and final mission by Winston Churchill – to be the official British observer on the raid that dropped the atom bomb on Nagasaki. Leonard Cheshire went on, in peace, to earn lasting fame as the founder of the Cheshire Homes for the chronically sick and disabled, for which he joined the exclusive ranks of the Order of Merit and the House of Lords. He is famously quoted as saying 'Peace is not just the absence of war'. Leonard Cheshire and Melvin Young were destined to serve together in the early part of their RAF careers in the Second World War.

Melvin's student years were not entirely devoted to law, rowing and flying. Notably he was visited by two of his American friends in 1935, Ed Rawson (then at Harvard) and Dudley Johnson. They spent the summer of 1935, in Ed's words, 'wandering around the south of England' and, it seems, a bit of

Wales. Melvin had a car, which Ed described as being of dubious vintage, and they used this to visit Oxford, Stratford-upon-Avon, Land's End, St Ives, Stonehenge, Bristol and Harlech Castle, staying in pubs on the route. Ed recalls that the car broke down one night, resulting in a stay at a bed-and-breakfast establishment in a small town. The proprietor had two teenage daughters and once they learned that Melvin had lived in Los Angeles, they pestered him about the Hollywood celebrities and were puzzled by his disdain for the topic and inability to give them any answers!

During this trip the boys visited Melvin's 'aunts', Ethel and Bert – Mrs Reginald Martin and her sister, Melvin's godmother, Miss Alberta Gearing. Ethel had a fine house at Tunbridge Wells, and Ed recalls that one morning he came down for breakfast and found two newspapers, *The Times* and the *Daily Express*; finding *The Times* rather dull he was avidly absorbing the more exciting *Express*, when Aunt Bert came in and explained to him 'Edward dear, that newspaper is meant for the servants' – an insight into the differences between the generations and, perhaps, across the Atlantic.

In 1936, Melvin took his sister Mary on a tour of Scotland. Hopefully the car was more reliable on this occasion. In the summer of 1938, members of the Oxford crew, with other oarsmen, went on a rowing trip to Germany. There is little information available about this expedition, but Melvin, Con Cherry and Frank Waldron went, along with several others. It seems to have been a fairly casual arrangement whereby a small nucleus formed the basis of a party who departed and returned together. A number of others joined in as their family commitments permitted. There seem to have been no officials of the university or the colleges included, just the student oarsmen. There is a group photograph (by a Nazi flagpole, beers in hand) and one looking down from a bridge on an eight in action, both possibly taken at Bad Ems by a photographer from Frankfurt-am-Main. This trip may be the basis of the story recounted, possibly with some artistic licence, by Richard Hillary in *The Last Enemy*. The British rowers came back with the 'Hermann Goering Trophy' which caused some embarrassment to Frank Waldron when war broke out – it did not sit well on his mantelpiece at Trinity and was hurriedly sent to the German Embassy.

It was during his time at Oxford that Melvin was introduced to Freemasonry by his friend and former schoolteacher 'Bill' Franklin, by then the Reverend A.H. Franklin. Freemasonry describes itself as one of the world's oldest secular fraternal societies – a society concerned with moral and spiritual values. Members are taught the rules of Freemasonry by a series of ritual dramas that follow ancient forms and use stonemasons' customs and tools symbolically. Bill Franklin's influence must have been considerable (as is often the case with teachers), because Angela recalls that their father disapproved of Freemasonry. Melvin normally held his father in great respect so his decision to become a Freemason is interesting. At this time, in 1937, he was naturally developing considerable independence of mind and the appeal of a mutually supportive brotherhood may well have been increased by the tension between his parents.

Whatever the reasons, on 3 February 1938, Henry Melvin Young was admitted to the Westminster and Keystone Lodge, No. 10, at a ceremony at the Grosvenor House Hotel; he was proposed by the Worshipful Master of the Lodge, Arthur Harrington Franklin and seconded by Brother O'Malley. A year later, Conrad Cherry was initiated into the same lodge, proposed by Brother Franklin, now the Immediate Past Master, and by Brother H.M. Young. Melvin continued to attend meetings for some years thereafter, as his duties permitted, and he left a sum of money to the lodge in his will for the purchase of a piece of silver. A fine silver bowl, suitably inscribed, is kept at the Freemasons Hall to this day.

Last but not least, Melvin was visited in Oxford on more than one occasion by Ed Rawson's sister Priscilla. Priscilla Rawson, who was six years older than Melvin, was a graduate of Bryn Mawr where she had studied music and literature. Several times in the 1930s, Priscilla came to England during the winter to further her musical studies. Melvin's father, Henry, escorted her to visit Melvin at Oxford; such were the proprieties of the day. It seems that the relationship between Melvin and Priscilla developed during those visits.

On leaving Oxford, Melvin spent much of his time with Aunt Bert at the apartment in Kensington, where she kept a room for him. He continued as a student of Gray's Inn and spent many hours on the river with Con Cherry. His tutor at Trinity, Philip Landon, also had a job for him; tutoring an Old Etonian oarsman called Alan Tyser. Landon was determined to maintain the success of the Trinity Eight on the river, and had identified Alan as a man to fill one of the places left vacant by those who, like Melvin, had left. Alan Tyser did not go up to Trinity until January 1939 and needed some coaching in law to get him up to speed – Melvin was recruited for this task over the Christmas period, and, of course, they rowed with Con Cherry at Putney. Alan Tyser sometimes ate and studied at Aunt Bert's large Kensington apartment; he recalled that she 'devoted herself to the benefit of Melvin'.

Alan Tyser had come from Eton with a reputation for adventure, based on an escapade in which he and several other senior boys chartered an aeroplane to take them to Le Touquet and back between the noon and 6 p.m. roll calls. The story of a near disaster boldly averted – they were initially refused permission for the return flight owing to the visit of the King and Queen to Paris – can be read in Ludovic Kennedy's autobiography, *On My Way to the Club*. Alan Tyser did indeed help the Trinity VIII to retain the Headship of the River; again Richard Hillary was the stroke and of that 1939 crew only three were to survive the war. Alan was commissioned into the Grenadier Guards, and served in their 1st and 4th Battalions, which became part of the Guards Armoured Division. He was seriously wounded in Normandy while on a reconnaissance mission. He remained a stalwart supporter of Trinity College all his life and remembered Melvin Young with affection as a great friend. Alan Tyser died on 20 October 2005, aged eighty-five.

Notes
1. High Street, the main thoroughfare through Oxford.
2. Letter H.M. Young to Father Sill, 3 September 1934.
3. Letter from H.M. Young to Father Sill, 28 May 1938.

Chapter 5

RAF – Training, Whitleys and Ditchings

Melvin joined the Royal Air Force Volunteer Reserve (RAFVR) and was commissioned as a Pilot Officer, General Duties Branch, on 13 September 1938. At this time the European political situation was very tense and war seemed a real possibility. Thanks to his training in the OUAS, he had some forty hours flying experience, roughly the requirement for a modern Private Pilots Licence and this entitled him to a Civil 'A' Licence. As an officer in the RAFVR he might have had access to some further training, but it seems he achieved little, if any. War was eventually declared against Germany on 3 September 1939 and, on 25 September, Melvin reported to No. 1 Initial Training Wing at Cambridge, where under the terms of a prior arrangement between the Air Ministry and Cambridge University, some nine colleges were made available as training establishments. His commanding officer was Wing Commander J.M. Mason, DSC DFC.

No. 9 Service Flying Training School

According to AP1388 (5th Edition, Sept 1939) 'RAF Standard Syllabus for Training of Pilots, Air Observers and Air Gunners' the Initial Training Wing would normally take eight weeks and cover Drill, Air Law, Armament, PT etc. However, given his OUAS and RAFVR experience, it is not surprising under the circumstances that this was cut to two weeks and Melvin was posted to No. 9 Service Flying Training School at Hullavington in Wiltshire on 7 October 1939. The commanding officer of

9SFTS at the time was Group Captain C.H. Elliot-Smith AFC. The sad record that Sergeant K.E. Sharman died at Hullavington that day as a result of a flying accident in an Audax aircraft was a warning of hazards to come. No. 14 Course started that day, with fourteen officers and eighteen airmen; all were in the RAFVR and were noted as having 'considerable flying experience'. Four courses were running at Hullavington at any one time.

The syllabus called for eight weeks on the Intermediate Training Squadron (ITS), flying Hart trainers, Audax and Anson aircraft. This was to be followed by eight weeks on the Advanced Training Squadron (ATS), using similar aircraft with the addition of the Fury (perhaps for the bombing and gunnery school at Penrhos). Each Squadron had two flight groups of two flights (it seems that Melvin was in 'E' Flight). In the event, the winter of 1939/40 was very severe with heavy rain and freezing conditions. Temperatures of minus 10 degrees Celsius frequently stopped all movements and the airfield was often unserviceable due to rain after frost. February 1940 was recorded in the 9SFTS Record book as being 'very bad for flying training due to weather'. All courses were extended by two to three weeks and so No. 14 course was not completed until 11 April, although some pupils (in Group II, see below) were posted away a week earlier; in Melvin's case to RAF Abingdon on 6 April for operational training on the Armstrong Whitworth Whitley bomber.

It seems that Melvin's flying training was not ultimately delayed by a spell, from 12 December to 23 December 1939, in the hospital at RAF Yatesbury, that windswept station on the Wiltshire Downs. The cause of his hospitalization is not recorded. However, his sister, Angela, remembered that he had injured a leg in 'some sort of RAF physical exercise' and this had not healed properly, requiring proper treatment. This may have been the same injury which he mentioned when writing again to Father Sill[1] this time from RAF Hullavington:

Dear Pater,
    I am spending Palm Sunday in bed, as I have the last few days with a slightly poisoned leg, a bruise of the bone from

playing football, the Association game, much against my
wishes one day some weeks ago when the aerodrome was
unserviceable. My protests that I did not know one end of a
football from the other were ignored and a kick which hurt
a lot at the time seemed to produce no bruise at all but
recurred in an infection some days ago, which I think has
been caught in time and brought to the surface. This
afternoon it is going to be lanced in about an hour's time and
that should put it right. I hope so.

Clearly he preferred to take his exercise in a boat or on a horse.
  Melvin continued this letter to Father Sill with an outline of
his flying training:

I wrote you last, I believe, right at the beginning of my
training here last October. Now I am nearly at the end of my
course here and will probably leave in another three weeks
after a course that has lasted six months instead of the four
they had first expected. That has been partially due to the
extraordinary winter we have had which has held up all
flying for long periods, though actually this is a very fine
aerodrome and we here have done much better than many
other places, and another reason is I think that there is no
such great hurry in our training as had at first been expected.
The war has not gone as people imagined it would. There
has not as yet been the terrific war in the air and wastage of
pilots. Consequently all operational units are full and so are
the advanced training units to which we would go from
here. So are the Flying Training Schools like this, and as you
may read in our papers there is a blockage in training at the
moment and there has not been any great regret that an
exceptional winter has held up training a certain amount.
  When I wrote you last I was right at the beginning of my
course of learning to fly twin engined aircraft, technically
service types but really trainers and that for me meant practically learning entirely over again how to fly for I had done
a year's very casual flying in the Oxford Air Squadron (and
one fortnight's camp) in my last year that was rather
occupied with boating and the boat race, 18 months before.

So when I got here both I and my instructors were appalled at my rustiness at even the most elementary principles of flying, of turns etc. which I had forgotten the feel of in the correct bank. However that soon came back.

That course lasted till Christmas and was devoted entirely to learn flying service aircraft. After eight days very welcome Christmas leave we moved on to the Advanced Training Course with new instructors in another part of this station and I have found that part of the work much more interesting, as that is not so much being taught to fly as a general service training. We learn (in the twin engine flight) photography, gunnery from a free gun turret (with a camera gun here) bombing practice only over a camera obscura here and all of the syllabus of flying training schools in every country, but it is much more interesting work and of course we do the jobs both as pilot and as crew both because one won't always be pilot and also on the old principle that one never appreciates the difficulties of the other fellow's job until one has had to do it oneself. After having put up with a little casual or careless piloting when a bomb aimer or pho-tographer, and had a whole run spoilt, one is never so careful a pilot as the next time oneself.

Since we had to have a war, I am more than ever glad that I am in the air force. It is a happy healthy life while it lasts, and I have found some old friends and made many new ones and though I haven't yet had to face any of the conflict and killing of war, I am not frightened of dying if that is God's will and only hope I may die doing my duty as I should. In the meantime, I remain as cheerful, I think, as ever and try to keep others so.

AP1388 outlined the qualities looked for in pupils for single-engined and twin-engined aircraft types, and pilots at SFTS were divided into two groups:

Group I Single-engined types – Fighter, Army Co-operation, Torpedo Bomber, Single-engined Bomber, Fleet Air Arm.

Group II Multi-engined types – Multi-engined Bomber, Flying Boats, General Reconnaissance.

Pupils for single-engined types were expected to have 'Alertness – with an element of dash' and the following qualities:
    (a) Ability to co-ordinate hand foot and eye, i.e. to make a good front gun shot and pilot controlled bomber.
    (b) Ability to exploit manoeuvrability, i.e. a liking and aptitude for aerobatics.

Pupils for Twin-engined types needed the following qualities in temperament:
    (a) Cool, steady, tenacious
    (b) Stamina
    (c) Initiative
    (d) Power of leadership

and in flying aptitude:
    (a) Reliable instrument pilot
    (b) Flying accuracy of the sort required for efficient co-ordination between pilot and bomb-aimer in precision bombing.

It is no surprise, therefore, that Melvin was selected as a bomber pilot; indeed, he told his family that 'They won't make me a fighter pilot...but maybe just as well, because they only survive three weeks!' However, it is worth recording the Remarks column from his Record of Service under, 'Courses of Instruction, etc.':

Flying Training at No. 9 FTS 10/10/39 – 6/4/40. Ground subjects above average. An above average pilot attained by keen-ness and hard work. General handling of aircraft good. Should make a good sound service pilot. Above average officer qualities. A likeable personality and a very satisfactory pupil. Authorised to wear Flying badge w.e.f 14/2/40. Passed 79.3%.

Among Melvin's fellow students at 9SFTS was one former

member of the OUAS, Leonard Cheshire. The rest will no doubt
have been from a wide background, albeit all keen enough to
have joined the RAFVR. We are fortunate to have a glimpse of
some of these other characters from the menu card of the end-
of-course dinner for 'E' Flight, held at the Cross Hands Hotel on
2 April 1940, just two years after Melvin's winning row in the
Boat Race. The Cross Hands Hotel is at Old Sodbury, some eight
miles west of Hullavington, on a cross roads; no doubt some of
the course members will have had cars to drive there (Melvin
had a small car during the war, more reliable than the vehicle of
his student days, according to his sister). The hotel dates from
the fourteenth century and more recently achieved fame in 1981
when HM The Queen took refuge there from a blizzard.

It would seem that the full effects of wartime economy had not
quite reached Old Sodbury by April 1940; the menu ran to five
courses with sole and duckling. The menu card was embellished
with 'thumbnail' sketches of twenty-three attendees, all of
whom had signed the reverse of Melvin's copy. The sketches, by
Jack Carter (clearly a talented cartoonist as well as one of the
course) show Melvin sitting in his favourite cross-legged
position, saying 'Stop that' – perhaps an indication that he may
have been a steadying influence on some of the wilder elements.
They also show one member sailing a boat and Leonard
Cheshire entering a pawnbrokers with a pair of skis (perhaps
trying to pay off his remaining gambling debts from Oxford
days). Mostly the reverse of the card is occupied by signatures,
but one comment says 'Many a battle fought but: – Trinity Boat
sunk', suggesting that Melvin had done his share of arguing
with his colleagues. The memory of the course and its members
was sufficiently valuable to Melvin for him to include it in his
photograph album.

Leonard Cheshire later recalled Melvin in these days[2] saying
that he had a wonderful outgoing, cheerful nature, and:

Somehow he always seemed to be in good form and was
immensely popular with everyone. He enjoyed playing
bridge and we used to have many a game together in the
Mess while waiting to go up to Flights. He was also very
intelligent and cultured, read a great deal and so was a very

good and interesting conversationalist. So far as I can remember he was a good pilot, certainly above average, and threw himself heart and soul into training.

Melvin was promoted to Flying Officer with effect 13 March 1940 (gazetted 14 May). His time at Hullavington had coincided with what has become known as 'The Phoney War', when apart from actions at sea such as the defeat of the German pocket battleship *Graf Spee* off Uruguay and the losses of two major British ships, *Courageous* and *Royal Oak* to U-boat torpedoes, there had been little action on the western front in Europe. This was about to change with the German attacks on Denmark and Norway, followed by Holland, Belgium and France.

However in the meantime there was a semblance of normal life. In his letter to Father Sill[3] Melvin recounted the 'substitute Oxford v Cambridge boat race' held at Henley on 2 March 1940, which he had been able to attend along with many old rowing friends that he had not seen since the war started. There was a gathering of many generations at the Leander Club, the younger ones in uniform who had 'scrounged leave from all parts of the country and some from France'. Among these was his great friend Conrad Cherry who had three days leave from a destroyer in the North Sea and who had become engaged to Glory Rowe, the sister of one of the winning Oxford crew in 1937.

The boat race had not been held at Henley since 1829. The course was that of the Olympic regatta of 1908, much shorter than the traditional Thames tideway course, but the 'scratch crews' had had little chance to practise. Melvin commented that the Great Western Railway had failed to anticipate the large crowds who turned up, and that there were more people than for a Regatta Final, with traders selling Dark and Light Blue ribbons and favours. Petrol rationing did not seem to have stopped many from coming by car. He described the crowd as 'an assorted one, rowing enthusiasts, many who always go to the boat race, many out for Saturday afternoon, and it had a Putney flavour with evacuee children and their parents on the towpath' and added:

As one paper said 'As a Boat Race it was a fine RAF display' for there were I think 19 service aircraft of all sizes and shapes circling round including three from here and a Spitfire looking very silly trying to go slowly not very successfully, with some large bombers for company.' The downside for Melvin was that the Cambridge crew won the race!

It seems that, when his duties permitted, Melvin would return to Oxford and help to coach the student oarsmen who had yet to be called up for war service. In his post-war appreciation of lost Oxford men *Tribute to Seven*, Ian Thomson wrote of Melvin:

> He kept reappearing at Oxford, either to coach a boat or cheer on a crew in a race for no other reason than to be there and see his friends. One came to take it as a matter of course that he was having an eventful war, not because he sought it, but because these things somehow came his way.

One can imagine him on the river bank at Oxford in the period 1939 to 1941, in winter muffled up against the cold in his thick Trinity College Boat Club scarf, blue with embroidered Trinity Griffons. This scarf resides in the Trinity archives to this day – after his death it was donated by his family for the use of future members.

We have a glimpse into Melvin's religious feelings at this time, again from his letter to Father Sill.[4] He says he intended to take confession, for the first time since leaving Kent eight years previously, before an Easter Communion. He said he had been feeling 'much happier in life recently', although not sure why. He commented that 'an English school is very negatively religious particularly Westminster with the intellectual socialism of the Abbey, and Oxford provides many distractions intellectually and otherwise for lack of devotion'. Melvin continued 'whether it being leaving Oxford or more probably the war I do feel more at peace with myself in my duty to God'. He had, he said, in recent months 'fallen under the spell' of Father (Dom) Bernard Clements, O.S.B. (Order of Saint

Benedict) the vicar of All Saints, Margaret Street, London, whom he described as magnificent.

William Dudley Clements (1880-1942) was vicar of All Saints from 1934 until his death from appendicitis in 1942. He was a big man, both physically – well over six feet tall and weighing over 20 stones, 280lbs – and in personality; in his earlier years he was, by his own admission, forthright and sometimes irascible. Educated at Pembroke College, Cambridge and Trinity College, Dublin, he worked for a few years as a school teacher before ordination as a priest in the Church of England in 1909. In 1911 he became a chaplain in the Royal Navy, and harangued the Admiralty to encourage more active religious observance by the sailors; the admirals were unmoved. After a period as chaplain of a training ship and as vicar at Portsea, in 1921 he took monastic vows, adopting the name Bernard, and joined the small Benedictine house at Pershore which later moved to more spacious accommodation at Nashdom Abbey, Burnham, Buckinghamshire. For five years (1926-1931) Dom. Clements was rector of St Augustine's Theological College at Kumasi, in the Gold Coast Colony, now Ghana. He described these years as the happiest of his life which gave him strong views against any racial intolerance. On his return to England he was called on to preach in many places and soon became a frequent speaker on radio, which was rapidly becoming the communication medium of the time, and became well known as a consequence. In 1934 the Bishop of London invited him to become the vicar of All Saints, for which he was suited by his strong Anglo-Catholic views. So, in 1939, with his ministry at its peak, he was well placed to influence Melvin in his post Oxford period, living with Aunt Bert in Kensington. It has been written[5] that Dom Bernard Clements' great power and ability lay in his intense interest in every person with whom he came into contact – 'His hearers thought with him because he appeared to be thinking with them.'

All Saints, which is but two streets back from the bustle of Oxford Street, London's principal shopping location, was designed by the famous architect William Butterfield, and was the pioneer building of the High Victorian phase of Gothic

Revival – its interior is particularly lavish. The foundation stone was laid by Dr Pusey on All Saints Day (1 November), 1850, and the church was consecrated by the Bishop of London in 1859.[6]

This church was part of the 'Oxford Movement' which, beginning in the 1830s, had attempted to stir the established Church of England into reviving certain Roman Catholic doctrines and rituals, led by notable clergymen such as Pusey, Keble and John Henry Newman – the last also a Trinity Man and destined to become a Roman Catholic Cardinal. The Oxford movement has exerted a great influence, doctrinally, spiritually and liturgically not only on the Church of England but also throughout the Anglican Communion.[7] Perhaps it is no coincidence that Melvin had become a Freemason two years earlier. Although Freemasonry is secular it has abundant rituals and mystic symbolism.

We also learn of Melvin's views on the war from this letter.[8] Whatever the mistakes in British policy that may have contributed to the war he was clear that it was a fight against extermination as a free people, even before the German invasion of western Europe which was yet to come. He felt that peace proposals from the American president would only give Germany a breathing space – like many in Britain he was probably unaware that we needed this breathing space at least as much as they did. He recounts that on a wet afternoon a few weeks previously he had managed to get over to Oxford to listen to Lord Halifax deliver a public lecture in the Sheldonian Theatre, where Oxford graduates receive their degrees. At that time Neville Chamberlain was still the Prime Minister and Halifax was the Foreign Secretary, as well as being the Chancellor of Oxford University, in which capacity he spoke that day. Melvin described Halifax as a statesman rather than a politician and thought it a very good address. Lord Halifax' chief points were 'that what frightened him was not that youth did not see eye to eye with old age (that was only natural) but that German youth had such a totally different outlook to us on everything…if we lost and not until we won could we set about thinking and arranging for a better order of things.' Melvin concluded this part of his letter 'He has a great brain and great ideals and is a very devout churchman, very much now I think the church militant after having done all he could to avoid war.'

Melvin ended his letter with news of his mother, Fannie, who had been seriously ill and had asked that he might try to visit her in California. Melvin was clearly much concerned by this and had applied to be posted temporarily to Canada to give him a chance to see her, but he had little expectation that this would be possible. It is clear that Melvin was very attached to both his parents and their separation was a source of great pain to him, as it was to his sisters. His obvious concern in March 1940 is in some contrast to the letter which he must have written some months earlier at the start of the war and left for his father 'Not to be opened till after my death' – in this he clearly felt that his mother had not behaved decently to any of them, least of all his father, and hoped that 'she may become sane again…and undo the harm that she has done and that you and she, Punkie (Mary) and Angela can all live happily together again.' Eventually Melvin was able to visit his mother in 1942, when posted to the USA and took his new bride, Priscilla, to see her. Fannie Young survived until 1955.

Whitleys

The Armstrong Whitworth Whitley was designed and built as a twin-engined, long range, night bomber to a 1934 Specification, B3/34. It was intended to be an interim design until more ambitious four-engined aircraft should become available, but continued in front line service as a bomber until 1942 and did further sterling service as a parachute troop transport, glider tug and anti-submarine patrol aircraft. The Whitley had a curious appearance. Its thick wing, set at a high angle of incidence on the fuselage, gave it a 'nose-low' attitude when flying, this being quite marked at maximum speed; but the bonus of this wing was that it permitted relatively slow take-off and landing speeds, a blessing in case of ditching. The earlier marks of the Whitley were seriously underpowered, but by the Mark V – the type in front line service by 1940 – the installation of Rolls-Royce Merlin engines had improved the performance considerably, albeit still marginal in some circumstances. It had the merit of being straightforward to fly, stable and easy to trim, but rather slow with cruising speeds in the range of 110 to 130 mph Indicated Airspeed. It was of rugged all-metal construction – Leonard Cheshire won an immediate DSO for continuing a raid over Germany after an anti-aircraft shell set off a flare inside his aircraft on the approach to the target, causing a very large hole in the side of the machine; nonetheless he bombed his target and the aircraft held together until they returned to base. The Whitley was designed for a crew of five; pilot(commander), co-pilot (who also acted as navigator), a wireless operator (who might also act as a gunner if necessary), a bomb-aimer/front gunner and a tail gunner.

Thus on 6 April Melvin was posted to No. 10 Operational Training Unit (OTU) in the familiar setting of RAF Abingdon with its neo-classical principal buildings, again in the company of Leonard Cheshire among others. At Abingdon, which is very close to Oxford, Melvin would have had opportunities to visit Trinity again, albeit briefly. The Station Commander at Abingdon when they arrived was Group Captain Martin Massey, a veteran of the First World War. Later, shortly before a posting to the USA, Group Captain Massey opted to make 'one last trip', was shot down and became a prisoner of war. In the late spring of 1940 Air Commodore William MacNeece Foster became the Base Commander at Abingdon and it fell to him to discipline Leonard Cheshire for some unguarded remarks – he did this with commonsense and discretion, thus saving the flying career of the man who was destined to become Britain's most decorated bomber pilot.[9]

The training on the Whitley at Abingdon took place against a background of crisis in Europe. On 10 May, the day on which the Germans struck west, thus ending the 'Phoney War', Air Chief Marshal Sir Edgar Ludlow-Hewitt, the Inspector General of the RAF and formerly the chief of Bomber Command, made a visit of inspection to 10 OTU.

Denmark, Norway, Holland, Belgium and France fell to the Germans during Melvin's two months' learning to fly the Whitley by day and night. Before he finished, soldiers were practising the defence of Abingdon itself, and the British

Expeditionary Force had been evacuated from Dunkirk. Many aircraft, including a few of the remaining Fairey Battles from the Advanced Air Striking Force, staged back through Abingdon after the debacle in France. On 26 May, the King called for a Day of National Prayer and there was a Combined Church service in one of the Abingdon hangars. Two days later Melvin's former room-mate, Paul Cooke, by then a Second Lieutenant in the Oxford and Buckinghamshire Light Infantry, died in the desperate retreat to Dunkirk – the war was getting close.

Despite the critical war situation Melvin felt compelled to write again to Father Sill, whom he had just learned had suffered a stroke, wishing him a complete recovery.[10] He commented, '...my training is now very nearly ended and I expect in a couple of weeks or so to be somewhat busier and may not have much time for writing'. He mentioned that he was only seven miles from Oxford at the station where he had his initial flying training with the University Air Squadron – indeed his letter was on RAF Abingdon notepaper, so censorship must have been minimal. He also mentioned that he had been able to lunch at the Leander Club at Henley the previous Sunday (12 May). The two central paragraphs of this letter are worth quoting in full as a guide to his feelings and views, and to show that he had a sound appreciation of world affairs:

> I believe I may have told you before, my flying is somewhat like my rowing, extremely clumsy, and so I have found heavy bombers more my type than light fighters, and though I shall probably, I suppose be flying chiefly at night am not displeased with the prospect and think that will suit me as well as anything. The future is appalling in its uncertainty for the world and our civilization and the fate of the individual a very minor matter even for that person. In any event I am not worried about [it] and do firmly believe, though it sounds a platitude that if we trust in God the right will prevail. That belief has made me much happier in recent months, nor can I really believe that our cause is not the right one, though I suppose every nation at war always thinks that.
>
> Our papers seem to be telling us – I don't know whether it

is wishful thinking or no – of a change of heart in the American people and of a greater readiness of a great nation to realize its responsibilities for civilisation. Today the President is delivering a message to Congress, which I hope to hear broadcast this evening.[11] Whatever his domestic policies, I am sure he is one of America's greatest statesmen (as well as a politician) and feel it would be calamitous if he were not re-elected, but of course, as so few Englishmen realize, who know nothing of the mysteries of the American Constitution, all action is pretty well impossible in Election year, which the Germans will doubtless have not forgotten.

The 'sharp end' of the training involved nine days armament training at Jurby, on the north-west corner of the Isle of Man. This training included dive- and stick-bombing, low level attack and defence against fighters. The weather in that period was excellent and the course was busy over the coastal bombing range attacking floating targets from various levels, singly and in formation. In Andrew Boyle's book *No Passing Glory*, Leonard Cheshire is reported as writing home from Jurby:

> It's a funny place here. It looks dead from the neck upwards, but the scenery is very lovely. The aerodrome is just under-neath a range of high hills which remind me of Scotland, and the sea is only a few yards away. As far as amenities go, there aren't many. Papers come a day late, letters probably don't arrive at all, beds are as hard as iron, if not harder, and there is nowhere to go after duty. Still if that's all there is to complain of, one can call oneself pretty lucky these days.

Melvin's first operational posting came on 10 June 1940, the day that Italy declared war on Britain and France, to 102 (Ceylon) Squadron, 4 Group Bomber Command, based at Driffield, a small market town in the Yorkshire Wolds, some twelve miles from the North Sea at Bridlington. The 102 Squadron motto reads *TENTATE ET PERFICITE* and the crest shows a winged lion on a globe holding a bomb. The Commanding Officer of 102 Squadron was Wing Commander S.R. Groom and Melvin's flight commander was Squadron Leader Philip R. (Teddy) Beare

DFC, with whom Melvin was destined to serve in the Middle East and to become a firm friend. Once more the Oxford connection survived, because Leonard Cheshire was also posted to 102, as well as Pilot Officer A.C.L. Akroyd-Stuart, who had graduated in law from Trinity College in 1939. Akroyd-Stuart, the son of an engineer, was born in Western Australia and educated at Lancing College in Sussex; he was also to become a Squadron Leader, was killed serving with 76 Squadron on 31 August 1943, and is buried at Roermond in Holland.

The 102 Squadron Operations Record Book (ORB) states that Melvin reported to the unit on 10 June from 78 Squadron, this being the 4 Group reserve squadron at Linton-on-Ouse which acted as a training squadron and a reservoir of crews. However there is no reference to 78 Squadron on Melvin's RAF Record of Service.

RAF Driffield had been used by the Royal Flying Corps in the First World War. When the RAF was expanded in the 1930s, in response to the deteriorating international situation, Driffield was chosen as one of the fourteen sites in the north-east of England for airfield construction. Indeed it was the first of the Expansion Programme aerodromes in Yorkshire to be opened, on 30 July 1936. It was equipped with five brick built 'C Type' hangars and the standard range of accommodation and technical buildings. Such was the quality of the Expansion Period RAF bases, with officers' messes designed by Lutyens, that many are still in use today, laid out on essentially the same pattern – Driffield however is no longer one of them, despite its distinguished wartime service.

102 Squadron had carried out a leaflet dropping sortie on the second night of the war and undertook its first bombing attack when one of the Whitleys bombed the German seaplane base at Sylt on the island of Hornum. This was in retaliation for a German raid on Scapa Flow, when bombs fell on a local village. With the Italian declaration of war, the squadron was soon in action south of the Alps; on 11 June seven of its Whitleys took part in a raid on the Fiat works in Turin, having refuelled at Jersey which was still in British hands, on the way. Many of

CERTIFIED COPY of an ENTRY
Pursuant to the Births and Deaths Registration Act 1953

Registration District St. George Hanover Square									
1915.		**Birth in the Sub-district of** Belgrave				**in the** County of London			
Columns:-	1	2	3	4	5	6	7	8	9	10
No.	When and where born	Name, if any	Sex	Name, and surname of father	Name, surname and maiden surname of mother	Occupation of father	Signature, description, and residence of informant	When registered	Signature of registrar	Name entered after registration
246	Twentieth May 1915 11A Lower Grosvenor Place	Henry Melvin	Boy	Henry George Melvin YOUNG	Fannie Forrester YOUNG formerly ROWAN	Second Lieutenant 4th Battalion Queen's Royal West Surrey Regiment (a Solicitor)	Henry M. Young Father 11A Lower Grosvenor Place Belgravia	First July 1915	L.C. Monnstephen Registrar	

Certified to be a true copy of an entry in a register in my custody.

_____ Deputy _____ Superintendent Registrar

25-6-03 Date

Copy of Melvin Young's birth certificate.

Melvin Young's birth place. 11 Lower Grosvenor Place, London.

Fannie Rowan, competing in the Southern California Tennis Championships, at the Virginia Hotel, Long Beach, c.1910.

Rowan Building, 5th and Spring, Los Angeles, c.1920. Also known as the Title Insurance Building for its principal tenants. (The Parkinson Archives).

Henry Young, in Army Captain's uniform with young Melvin, c.1918.

Melvin, age 5, Los Angeles.

Melvin horse riding, Eastbourne Sands, 1922.

Melvin with Aunt Floss
(Miss Florence Rowan),
California, c.1925.

Melvin at Amesbury
School, c.1925.

Melvin with his sister
Angela in her pram,
London, c.1926.

Melvin, standing, with
friend, Round Pond,
Kensington, London,
c.1927.

Melvin, c.1927, already developing the reading habit.

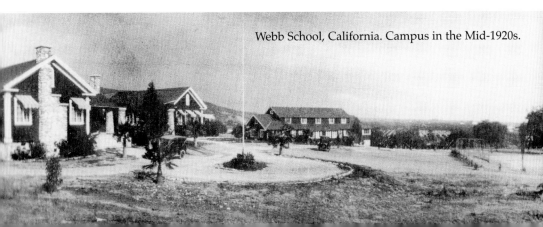

Webb School, California. Campus in the Mid-1920s.

Melvin on horseback in California, 1929. Probably at Webb School.

Melvin at Kent School.
(Kent School).

Kent School 'Old Main' Building. (Author, 2005)

Father Sill, Order of the Holy Cross. Founder Headmaster of Kent School, Connecticut. (Kent School)

Melvin, 'Bill' Franklin
and Priscilla Rawson in
Connnecticut, June 1932.

Melvin bathing at
Littlehampton,
England 1933.

Melvin wrote to Father Sill
(known to his pupils as 'Pater')
from RMS *Majestic*, crossing
from the USA to England
during April 1933.

Riding with 'Aunt Ethel', Mrs Reginald Martin, 1933.

Melvin Young at
Westminster School,
July 1934.

Melvin's room over
the Chapel Arch,
Trinity College,
Oxford. (Author, 2004)

Trinity College front
quadrangle, from Melvin's
room over the Chapel Arch.
Trinity 'Cottages' at far side
of Quad. (Author, 2004)

Melvin on holiday in England with Edward Rawson, 1935.

Melvin meets a kitten on holiday, 1935. This was one of Priscilla's favourite pictures of Melvin.

Trinity College, Oxford, 1936 Coxswainless Four. Michael Rowe, Melvin Young, Frank Waldron and Sir John Worsley-Taylor, Bt; Con Cherry (centre) Coach.

Philip Landon - Law Tutor and Fellow of Trinity College, Oxford, 1920-1956. (Trinity College, Oxford)

Melvin sculling through a lock on the River Thames.

Trinity College, Oxford, 'Head of the River' Crew, 1938. Melvin seated at the left of the picture. (Trinity College, Oxford)

Conrad Cherry, President of the Oxford University Boat Club, 1938. Melvin's close friend and fellow oarsman.

these aircraft were unable to negotiate the Alps, due to icing conditions and thunderstorms. It was standard procedure at that time for newly trained pilots to serve as second pilot for a period in order to familiarize themselves with operations. Thus Melvin's first operational sortie was with Pilot Officer J.F. Painter as his skipper on 19/20 June, attacking marshalling yards at Schwerte, near Dortmund in the Ruhr.

Melvin's next operation with Pilot Officer Painter was in Whitley V, N1415 'DY-D' with a crew consisting of Sergeant E. Burke (observer/bomb aimer), Sergeant D. Parr (wireless operator) and Flight Sergeant D.E.J. Clark (air gunner). The target was an aircraft factory at Hamburg and they were airborne for nearly seven hours. They reported attacking from 10,000ft, dropping two sticks of bombs, eight of which were observed to burst. The weather was good over the target, with some cloud and a low haze, and they experienced considerable heavy and light flak. At this period in the war, bomber command crews had to rely on their own navigation to find the target; they had no radio guidance aids and Pathfinder squadrons were still in the future. It is not surprising that they were often uncertain of their position and mistaken in the identification of targets.

After this first raid, up to 24 August, Melvin flew on some thirteen raids with Pilot Officer Painter to attack a range of targets: Kiel where their objective was the battlecruiser *Scharnhorst*, which they failed to find and so brought their bombs back, Emden, Paderborn, Bremen, Kassel, Hamburg, Düsseldorf, twice, once unsuccessfully, bombs brought back, Frankfurt which was also unsuccessful, Milan, where an enormous fire was started, Augsburg -'bombs on target' – and the Daimler-Benz factory at Stuttgart. The Luftwaffe tried to get its own back on Driffield, attacking at night on 19 June. Although some fifty bombs were dropped, no hits were recorded on the aerodrome or its buildings.

However, it was during this period, at the height of the Battle of Britain, that Driffield suffered the heaviest raid on a British bomber station of the entire war, and was put out of action until early in 1941. On 15 August the RDF (Radar) station at nearby

Staxton Wold identified a force of incoming enemy aircraft and
Spitfires of 616 Squadron from Leconfield and Hurricanes of 73
Squadron from Church Fenton were sent to intercept. Some fifty
Junkers 88 aircraft from Aalborg in Denmark were heading for
Driffield which, being near the coast, was a tempting target.
Although the raiders suffered heavy losses and indeed were dis-
couraged from similar raids in future, enough got through to
cause heavy damage on the airfield, both bombing and strafing
with cannon and machine guns. Four of the five hangars were
badly damaged and many buildings set on fire. Twelve
Whitleys were destroyed, thirteen people killed and many
others wounded. The 102 ORB states that some thirty enemy
aircraft attacked at 13.20 hours and dropped 100 bombs. The
raid is well documented elsewhere, but Leonard Cheshire later
recalled being in an air raid shelter with Melvin who, to relieve
the tension, produced a pack of cards and asked, 'Anyone like a
game of bridge?' 102 Squadron was relocated to Leeming
(briefly) and then to Linton-on Ouse and eventually to Topcliffe,
all bases being of the familiar Expansion Period pattern.

On 13 August Melvin took part in his first raid on Italy, again
with Pilot Officer Painter as captain, and with Sergeants Binks,
Parr and Hird completing the crew. They reported that
enormous fires were started. Two years later, addressing the
boys at Kent School, in Connecticut, he recounted this
operation:

> The trip across the Alps was most beautiful. Flying across
> Germany we had been used to fighting it out, but in Italy we
> met no opposition. It seems that when the Italian anti-
> aircraft gunners heard us coming, they ran for the air raid
> shelters. So while the Italian Command was busy court-mar-
> tialling their soldiers, we managed to drop our load and slip
> away.

We may suspect that a degree of bravado had been slipped into
this account to encourage the youth of America. However he
repeated essentially the same story to RAF recruits training at
MacDill Airbase in 1942, attributing the story of Italian soldiers
deserting their posts to intelligence sources, which in turn may

have been trying to encourage the British at a very difficult period in the war. At MacDill he recounted that when flying over neutral Switzerland:

> We could look down and see the homes lighted up in the Swiss towns. It gave us a happy feeling, coming from a land that had been blacked out for a year.

Despite the tension of the times and the action, both at home and over enemy territory, there was time to relax. Leonard Cheshire provides a snapshot of a lighter moment in his book *Bomber Pilot*, first published in 1943. Cheshire describes how he and Melvin went bathing at the coast and how he was aided by a young girl as he was trying to sort the sand out of his socks and shoes. In the summer of 1940 the RAF were the heroes of the nation and young flyers were held in especial regard. Perhaps the famous Cheshire charm also worked its magic, for Melvin was left to towel his own feet!

There was much light hearted banter in the mess and some more serious discussion. Andrew Boyle's biography of Leonard Cheshire, *No Passing Glory*, says of Melvin that he was addicted to starting involved discussions on improbable subjects at a moment's notice, and that, perhaps because he was older, had an 'intuitive wisdom' which Cheshire lacked. A scene, which certain survivors of 102 Squadron recalled, is of Melvin, seated in his preferred cross-legged fashion on the mess floor, arguing with Cheshire. Richard Morris's biography *Cheshire* described Melvin as a widely read man in whose company Cheshire sparkled, and as a 'long standing friend who provided support in face of derisive comments about Oxford intellectuals'. But when winter came, Melvin and Leonard Cheshire were not above taking part in snowball fights and sliding on the ice.

Convoy Patrol and the First Ditching

On 1 September 1940, 102 Squadron moved temporarily to Prestwick, under 15 Group Coastal Command, to provide convoy escort for shipping in the Atlantic, the presence of covering aircraft being one of the best ways to counter the U-boat menace. Melvin now became an aircraft commander, and his first operation as such was on 9 September, in Whitley DYG, with Pilot Officer Weizman (second pilot), Pilot Officer Forsdyke (observer), Sergeant Hird (wireless operator/air gunner) and Sergeant Burns (air gunner). This trip took from 09.30 until 16.45. Such trips continued through September with some aircraft being detached to operate from Aldergrove in Northern Ireland.

It was on a flight from Aldergrove, on 7 October 1940 in Whitley DY-P P4995, that the first of Melvin's ditchings occurred. The crew consisted of Sergeant Collier (second pilot), Pilot Officer Forsdyke, Sergeant Burns and Sergeant Hird. It was a day of moderate to good visibility with a west-south-west wind up to 20 mph. The ORB simply records: 'Force landed in sea due engine trouble. Crew picked up by ex-American destroyer HMS St Mary's after 22 hours in dinghy.' Of course there was more to it than this cryptic record tells.

The pilot's handling notes for the Whitley advise that in the case of engine failure it should be possible to maintain level flight with the sound engine at 2,600 rpm and +4 lbs of boost (or full throttle), flying at 110 mph, any bombs having been dumped. Ironically, it does warn that 2,600 rpm is not recommended because engine vibration 'causes high stress and possible fracture of the propeller blades'. Whatever the book said, Whitleys were known to have poor single engine performance and, starting from a low altitude Melvin found himself and his crew facing a ditching in short order. The relevant aircraft safety equipment consisted of life jackets for each crew member and a Type H dinghy stowed near the exit on the port rear side of the fuselage. From their brace positions the crew were expected to make their way to this exit, although the pilot had an outwardly opening crash exit above his seat from which he could emerge and move along the top of the fuselage to join the others in the dinghy. The dinghy was inflated automatically on ejection from the aircraft by a carbon dioxide gas cylinder. It had water ballast pockets underneath to maintain stability and a drogue to keep it steady in the wind and slow its drift, various lines to assist entry, a knife and bellows to keep the buoyancy topped up. It offered, however, very limited protection against the weather.

It is both fortunate and interesting that this nearly disastrous adventure was well recorded, both in Melvin's own words and by an American reporter, William L. 'Bill' White, who was travelling on the destroyer which rescued them. The ship, on its first voyage under the White Ensign as HMS *St Mary's*, was one of the fifty First World War four-funnel, flush-deck destroyers which President Roosevelt, after long consideration, agreed to transfer to the Royal Navy in exchange for bases in the Caribbean; the ships were given the names of towns common to both Britain and the USA and were thus referred to as the 'Town Class'. These ships began to be transferred to the British in September and as part of the 'delivery voyage' HMS *St Mary's* and several sister ships provided the surface escort for a convoy. Bill White was able to record the event in words and photographs for the American public – his report was published in *LIFE* Magazine on 2 December 1940.

Bill White was the son of William Allen White who was the owner of the *Emporia Gazette* in Kansas and who was known as the voice of the Midwest and small town America through his syndicated columns. Bill was convinced that Britain was fighting for democracy and that America should join the war, and was on his way to report on the war from Britain; the London Blitz in particular. His father believed that it was not America's war, but helping Britain was the best way of keeping the USA out of it. Bill White's account of the voyage describes a rough crossing with various alarms due to U-boat activity and aircraft sightings (mostly British, fortunately). Then after eleven days of tedium and relative discomfort and closing with the coast of Northern Ireland he went to the bridge after lunch and found the Captain scanning the sea through his binoculars with particular attention, having spotted a small object. The Captain ordered a change of course toward the object, which eventually turned out to be a dinghy containing five people. White recorded the actual rescue in these words:

Their raft is a huge orange doughnut, and within its circle five men are squatting, one of them frantically waving a canvas paddle aloft.[12] A minute more and they are abeam – hardly 50 yds away. As we sweep by they wave frantically and then sink dejectedly. But we are only manoeuvring to put our ship's bulk between the raft and the wind. In another two minutes we have turned and are coming back. Now our engines are off. We drift slowly toward them. Now they're just abeam. One fellow paddles frantically until the raft bumps the ship's side. Now our propellers boilingly backwater at the command and ropes go writhing down toward their grappling hands. A ship's ladder goes over our side.

But who are they? These staring, bleary-eyed men with salt-drenched blond hair, who sag weakly in the bobbing raft? 'Germans!' guesses one of our crew. 'We picked some of the blighters up last month. One of their aircraft came down.'

'Nah, they aren't!' says another Cockney scornfully. 'Look at the uniforms, will ye? They're no Jerries – that's our own RAF'. And so it is. The water-soaked horizon blue of the RAF under the orange life jackets – orange because it is the color most vividly contrasting with the sea's blue-green. Numb hands are now reaching up for our ropes. It is much too rough to launch a boat.

One of the aviators rises wildly, unsteadily grapples at a rope, is too weak to wrap it around him, topples into the sea. Instantly a sailor goes over our rail, comes up behind the man with the loose-rolling head and wild eyes just out of the water. He ties the rope under his arms and pushes him to the dangling ship's ladder.[13] But he's too weak to manage the rungs with his cold hands and feet, so three sailors pull his sea-chilled body up and over the side. The others with a little help from our sailors mount the wooden rungs and reach the solid safety of steel deck, and are half led, half carried down to the cozy warmth of our wardroom.

White goes on to tell how the rescued airmen were dried and warmed. At first they declined food, just wanting water and sleep. Melvin was photographed with the Captain (Lieutenant K.H.J.L. Phibbs), wearing clothes borrowed from Bill White; a splendid publicity photograph for the Admiralty. Indeed one of White's pictures, of almost portrait quality, remains the favourite image of Melvin among the Young family. It shows him smiling, and who would not have had a broad smile under the circumstances? HMS *St Mary's* was given permission to race on ahead of the convoy to 'a British port'[14] with the survivors who were collected at the dockside by RAF ambulances to take them to hospital for treatment and check-ups, before some well deserved 'survivors leave'. White was particularly pleased that he was reporting on the rescue of a crew led by an Anglo-American pilot, and we can forgive him the journalistic phraseology he felt his readers would appreciate.

Melvin's own story of the ditching and rescue has survived in various forms. He made a radio broadcast at 6 p.m. on the BBC Home Service on 31 October, entitled 'A rescue at Sea' by a Flying Officer (speaking anonymously) – the transcript has been kindly made available by the BBC, but the recording no longer exists. The same words appeared in *The War Illustrated* on 6 December entitled 'We were rescued by an American destroyer' and in the 1941 book *Winged Words – Our Airmen Speak for Themselves* (published by Heinemann), under the heading 'Rescue of an RAF Crew in the Atlantic, by a Flying officer.' It is worth quoting his story in full:

> Many people have said what a welcome addition the American destroyers would be to our fleet. I am sure that no one is likely to give them a more hearty and grateful welcome than that given by my crew and myself one afternoon a couple of weeks ago, when, after drifting aimlessly about in a rubber dinghy off the coast of Ireland for a very long time we suddenly saw on the crest of a wave the funnels of a destroyer.
>
> It happened like this: We had been detailed to escort a convoy and had met it inbound at about midday. Several hours later while we were still on patrol, the rear gunner reported a trace of smoke from the starboard engine. I could see very little myself; the oil and radiator temperatures were quite normal and I was not unduly worried. I decided, however, to return to base at once and the wireless operator reported to base that we were doing so. But almost immediately our trouble increased, the engine got very hot – and so

did I – and it was only a matter of a very few minutes before we found ourselves cooling rather rapidly in the Atlantic.

I saw clouds of smoke pouring from the engine, the temperatures shot right up, and I had to throttle the engine back to prevent it catching fire. We were only at about 500 feet at the time and the aircraft would not maintain height on the other engine. I told the crew to stand by for a landing in the sea, and our dinghy drill had to be carried out pretty rapidly. The tail gunner came forward to the dinghy, the second pilot and the navigator went aft, followed by the wireless operator after he had finished sending his SOS. They all braced themselves for the shock of hitting the water. This we must have done with quite a crack, in spite of my efforts to hold off as long as possible and reduce speed, as the fuselage broke nearly in two just forward of the leading edge of the wings. The cockpit immediately began to fill with water and I thought it was time for me to be moving. I climbed out through the escape hatch in the roof and found the rest of the crew in the sea with the dinghy which was just opening.

I scrambled across the gap in the fuselage and walked aft. The dinghy was fully open and the rope tying it to the aircraft had been cut but was still caught in the angle between the fuselage and tailplane so I was able to step straight into it. This was a great stroke of luck as the hardest job is usually to get the first man into the boat. We pushed ourselves clear of the aircraft and then I helped the crew in. The wireless operator was the most urgent case as he had hit himself jumping in and had swallowed a lot of salt water when he went under; he was very nearly unconscious. We got him in after quite a struggle and the rest of the crew came aboard in turn. The aircraft had sunk by the time the last had got in.

This happened at about four o'clock in the afternoon; there were about three hours of daylight remaining, and of course we hoped very much that our SOS would have been received and that we should be picked up or at least sighted that afternoon. We were at that time within sight of land, but a strong south-westerly wind was carrying us away out to sea. Darkness fell without a sight of ships or aircraft and we resigned ourselves to at least another fourteen hours afloat. At first we could see the beam from a lighthouse, but that disappeared by midnight, as the wind which was increasing nearly to gale force blew us farther from land.

There were only three things to do all night, to keep awake, to keep warm and to try to keep the boat as dry as possible. We had all, except the rear gunner, swallowed some salt water and were seasick. I was lucky and was not very bad, but some felt most unhappy inside all night and wanted very much to go to sleep. However we all kept awake and found three exercises which seemed the most practicable for keeping warm. First we would pat our hands briskly on our thighs, that warmed both hands and thighs and was our commonest exercise, which later in the night we did about every ten minutes. Then we did the 'cabman's swing' swinging our arms across our chests as taxi-drivers do on cold days, and we found that good for keeping the circulation going. Finally we smacked each other on the back. I must have been somewhat vigorous in this last exercise as my neighbour said it was too much like being hit by a pile-driver. We did our best to keep cheerful and as my watch was watertight and working I reported the time every half-hour and the number of hours to daylight. It was a great landmark at one in the morning when the night was half over and then six hours only to go.

I found also that I kept warm by baling out the water, which we did with my shoes. At first we shipped water quite often as the tops of the waves broke over us. Later, though the seas were steadily rising with the wind increasing through the night, we became quite expert at riding the huge Atlantic rollers, and found that with two of us facing into the wind and two with their backs to it we could watch the waves and by leaning away from the bad ones ease ourselves over the top of them without shipping water very often.

The night passed very slowly indeed. I had decided not to open the rations till morning as I knew we should be much

hungrier then. I am afraid I adopted rather a Captain Bligh
of the *Bounty* line over the rations as I wanted to make them
last for three days. Dawn crept upon us at about six-thirty
after an apparently interminable night of back-slapping and
wave-climbing. It was quite light by seven-thirty, and we
were out of sight of land, but suddenly to our joy we saw a
ship in the west. It got larger and was heading almost in our
direction; then it altered course and came straight for us. We
stood up in turn and waved and we all shouted, but she was
to windward and neither saw or heard us. We could see her
quite clearly and she passed within two or three hundred
yards and was, I think, a small armed merchantman. This
was a dreadful disappointment as we had practically
decided what we would have for breakfast; biscuits and
brackish water were a very poor substitute for bacon and
eggs. However as some slight consolation and to warm us
up I allowed us each a very small swallow from our rum
flask, which I was saving for emergencies.

We saw several aircraft during the morning, but even those
fairly near did not spot us because the sea was a mass of
white horses. About ten o'clock the rear gunner was washed
overboard by a wave breaking crossways over us, although
he was sitting on his hands holding the rope as we all did.
However, he kept his hold and we got him aboard again,
and did our best to warm him up with rum and exercise.

At midday there were more biscuits and Horlicks tablets
for lunch, but I don't think we were really hungry yet as
some of the crew wouldn't eat their biscuits. I told the crew
that we should probably have to spend another night in the
dinghy and they stayed remarkably cheerful; in spite of this
dreary prospect.

Suddenly about 2 pm we thought we saw some ships in
the distance. All morning, however, we had been seeing low
islands and lighthouses which proved to be merely the crests
of waves breaking in the distance, so I didn't have much
faith in any of these ships. Then we started looking round
again and to our joy saw from a crest of a wave a flotilla of
destroyers steaming towards us in line abreast. The second

pilot recognised the four funnels and flush deck of the American destroyers and we thought they would pass on either side of us. Then as they drew near they altered course away from us so that we passed to port of the port ship of the line. We held the rear-gunner[15] up and he waved our green canvas paddle. Just as we had about given up hope again we saw people waving from the decks and she turned in a circle round us.

Soon after she came alongside and threw us a line, at first shouting directions in German, as they had mistaken our uniforms. The ship was rolling heavily and when our navigator[16] caught hold of the rope ladder he could not get a foothold and as his hands were too cold to keep a grip he fell into the sea. A sailor at once jumped in, put a line round him and he was lifted out. The rest of the crew and myself were able to climb aboard. We were taken below and had our skin practically rubbed off us before we were wrapped in blankets and put in an officer's cabin, with tea and rum and hot food, all extremely welcome.

As soon as I was warm I borrowed some clothes and went on the bridge to thank the captain. I learned that it was he who had first spotted us when he saw through his glass our yellow skull-caps and life-saving jackets and dinghy, which he thought was some wreckage as we appeared and disappeared on the distant waves.

We were all made most abundantly welcome by the Navy and went ashore that night very happy men indeed.

This was the story as told to the general public at the time. In reality there had been a failure of the rescue alerting system. Two years later, speaking at Kent School, Melvin stated that:

The woman in the auxiliary at home who caught our [SOS] message somehow put it in the files, and while we all sat in our rubber boat, our distress signal lay resting in a file for future reference.

This is confirmed by a note dated 21 October from Air Vice Marshal A. Coningham (AOC.-in-C. of 4 Group) to Melvin (now back at Linton-on-Ouse) which reads:

My dear Young,

I was most interested to read your excellent report on the forced landing in the sea off Ireland.

2. You all had a very fortunate escape. The distress procedure is the subject of investigation in Coastal Command, but the sea conditions made things much more difficult.

3. Please convey to Sergt. Burns, who put up such a good show, my commendation for the excellent way he supported you.

4. I hope your crew are all well again and none the worse for a gruelling experience.

Yours sincerely

A Coningham'

On 10 October 102 Squadron had moved to Linton-on-Ouse, having finished their detachment to 15 Group Coastal Command and returned to 4 Group, and so this was the base from which Melvin returned to operations, until they moved on to Topcliffe on 16 November. However, while at Linton he took part in raids on Bremen (28 October) where a few small fires were started, Ruhland (10 November) where they also caused fires and set off for Berlin on 14 November, but returned after an hour and a half with an unserviceable compass.

From Topcliffe, his first operation was to Duisburg in company with a Whitley flown by Sergeant Rix; they reported a big explosion and fires. Then on 23 November, 102 joined with 77 Squadron (also based at Topcliffe) for a raid on the Royal Arsenal at Turin. The four aircraft from 102 Squadron attacked the primary target and the railway station, causing many explosions and large fires. But this raid cost five Whitleys, which failed to return due to fuel exhaustion, exacerbated by bad weather; three from 102 Squadron and two from 77 Squadron. Of the 102 Squadron aircraft, Sergeant Pearce force-landed near Shoreham, Sergeant Rix and his crew bailed out by parachute near Tangmere and Melvin ditched off Start Point in Devon; all the 102 Squadron crews were saved. Of the two 77 Squadron aircraft, one hit high tension cables trying to land in Suffolk and the other ditched off Dungeness, its pilot, Pilot Officer Bagnell, was rescued but the remainder of his crew were drowned.

The flying accident card (courtesy of the Air Historical Branch RAF) tells us that Melvin force landed DY-F (T4216) in the sea due to lack of fuel, having been unable to get a position fix due to an unreliable radio. The 'landing' was 'into wind, speed reduced, tail touching first'. The record card gives the time as 05.00 hrs, states that the aircraft sank and the crew were saved by dinghy. The record card also shows that at this time Melvin had accumulated 262 hours 'solo' on the Whitley, of which 154 were at night. The rest of the crew were Flying Officer F.G. Malim (second pilot), Sergeant R. Bristow (observer), Sergeant W. Craven (wireless operator) and Sergeant A.P. Clifford-Reade (air gunner). Sadly Craven, Clifford-Reade and Malim were destined to die in the next few months serving with 102 Squadron.

The 1942 Ministry of Information booklet *Air Sea Rescue* highlighted this ditching (albeit anonymously) as an ideal rescue. It tells us that:

The wireless operator had succeeded in sending an SOS which enabled the Whitley to be plotted some forty miles off Plymouth. There was a slight southerly wind, the sea was calm and there was little moon and no mist. The pilot made a successful tail down landing after switching on his landing lights. The dinghy was inflated without incident. All the crew scrambled aboard, the only mishap being an injury to the tail gunner, who broke his arm when the Whitley hit the water. They entered the dinghy at 4.30 in the morning. They were found by a Lysander, which had gone out at daybreak to search for them, at 10.05 hrs, five hours and thirty-five minutes after ditching. The Lysander approached them with the sun behind it and its pilot saw them easily. They had used Fluorescine, (a chemical substance which gives the sea around the dinghy a yellowish-green colour which shows up well from the air) as soon as daylight appeared. The launch arrived at 14.30 hours to pick them up.

The Lysander was from 16 Squadron, based at Weston Zoyland, Somerset, engaged in coastal patrol duties. However, two aircraft were detached to RAF Roborough (Plymouth Airport) for 'Rescue work at sea'. The 16 Squadron ORB records that the weather was fine and that four rescue flights were made on 24 November, thus:

Lysander III R9106 Flight	P/O Coombs, Sgt Morgan	R e s c u e 09.05-11.30
Lysander III R9110 Flights	P/O Gouge, Sgt Leach	R e s c u e 10.45-12.30
		13.00-14.00
		14.15-14.40

It would seem that these two aircraft found and kept watch on Melvin and his crew until the rescue launch arrived from Plymouth.

Not surprisingly Melvin then acquired the nickname 'Dinghy' – and sometime later a hoax was perpetrated, supposedly posting him to Calshot to run a dinghy training unit – he bought a round of drinks in anticipation of leaving 102 Squadron, before finding he was the subject of a joke! He was aware that his ditchings and background in rowing would be the subject of mess banter. Speaking to the boys at Kent School in 1942 he said:

> My reputation for always wanting to row is bad in the Air
> Force. Several times I have had to park my plane in the sea
> and take to the rubber boats. My friends cautioned me that
> it was a rather expensive way of brushing up on my rowing.

It was acknowledged that Melvin had taken all aspects of training very seriously, including dinghy drill, reflecting the personality that had persisted in getting his rowing to a high enough standard to win his Blue at Oxford.

The survival of Melvin and his crews in their two ditching incidents was only partly the result of good training and Melvin's insistence in practising dinghy drill – luck inevitably played its part. Sadly, luck was not with many other of the crews who came down in the sea.

In 1940 the Air Sea Rescue (ASR) organization was still developing and comprised an ad hoc collection of services – RAF launches in some places, RN launches, Lysander search aircraft, the Royal National Lifeboat Institution, and the fishing fleet. This was clearly not satisfactory so, in 1941, the Directorate of Air Sea rescue was formed and became more effective as the war progressed. By mid 1941 the recovery rate of aircrew had risen to 35 per cent. In 1943, with bombing operations much more intense by both the RAF and the USAAF, the Air Sea Rescue services had saved 1,684 aircrew out of 5,466 presumed to have ditched. Inevitably, there were numerous tragedies, and in many cases the story will never be told.[17]

A sad incident from 102 Squadron's history relates to a raid on Cologne on 1/2 March 1941. The Whitley flown by Squadron Leader Florigny was forced down in the North Sea in a gale during its return flight. The rest of the crew, including Pilot Officer R.C. 'Revs' Rivas, got into the dinghy, but it was swept away from the aircraft before Squadron Leader Florigny could get to it. He was last seen on the sinking fuselage and was feared drowned. The rest of the crew were picked up by a trawler after eight hours in the dinghy. This story is recounted by Rivas, who had often flown with Leonard Cheshire, in his book *Tail Gunner*, and also in Air Commodore Graham Pitchfork's book *Shot Down and in the Drink*. Tragically, Florigny's younger brother was also lost on the same raid to Cologne – both are commemorated on the Aircrew Memorial at Runnymede.

In December Melvin was back in action, raiding targets such as Mannheim, Mulheim, Merignac (Bordeaux Airport), Bremen, Wilhelmshaven, and Cologne. The attack on Merignac, in company with 102 Squadron aircraft flown by Cheshire and Verran, was aimed at the long range FW200 Kondor aircraft which caused much trouble for British convoys in the Atlantic. Melvin attacked from 8,000 ft putting bombs on the hangars. All three aircraft landed at Abingdon on return. Melvin's last operation with 102 Squadron was to Hanover on 10/11 February 1941.

Melvin would have been very much aware that Britain was under attack at night by the Luftwaffe at this time and, in particular, that his sister Mary was working as a nurse at St Bartholomew's Hospital throughout the London Blitz. The great fire storm of 29 December 1940, when St Paul's Cathedral was barely saved from destruction, raged all around the hospital. The news of the Blitz on London was relayed to the USA by several American journalists, including Bill White who had reported the rescue in October from HMS *St Mary's*. Melvin's American friends were concerned for his safety and that of his family. Clementine Rawson was in touch with Melvin's godmother, Alberta Gearing – living in Tunbridge Wells at the time – who reported that she thought Melvin 'looked older and worn'. Thus Clementine had heard of both his ditchings and was relieved to learn that all the Youngs (Henry, Melvin, Mary and Angela) 'were still alive at Christmas'. The bombing was bad but probably sounded worse on the other side of the Atlantic.[18] She passed on Melvin's address as being that of his father in Hertford.

During this period Melvin was promoted to Acting Flight Lieutenant on15 December 1940, a rank made substantive in 6 April 1941.[19] In May 1941 he was awarded the Distinguished Flying Cross (DFC) for his service with 102 Squadron. The citation, in the *London Gazette* on 9 May 1941 reads:

> This officer has carried out 28 bombing missions involving 230 hours flying as well as 6 convoy patrols on which some 40 hours were spent in the air. His operational flights include attacks on important targets in Germany and Italy. On two occasions he has been forced down on the sea, on one of which he was in the dinghy for 22 hours in an Atlantic gale. On both occasions his courage and inspired leadership, combined with a complete knowledge of dinghy drill, were largely responsible for the survival of his crews. He has always shown the greatest keenness to seek out and destroy his targets.

Although Melvin's parents were separated (indeed, unknown to him and his sisters at the time, they were divorced) he kept in touch with both of them. In the case of Fannie, his mother in California, by letter. Fannie was justifiably proud of Melvin's

DFC and an article appeared in a Pasadena newspaper, with a photograph of him in RAF uniform, entitled 'South Pasadena Flyer's "Bold Leadership in Raids on Germany" Wins British Honour'. It is a fine point that Melvin probably did not consider himself a native of Pasadena – Ed Rawson recalls that he thought of southern California as a desert and, in truth, it is semi-arid. Several books on the Dambusters have associated him with Pasadena, even stating he was born there! However Fannie's pride is understandable. The article stated that:

Flight Lieut. Melvin Young, 26, of the Royal Air Force has been awarded the Distinguished Flying Cross by King George VI of England. This announcement was verified yesterday by the flyer's mother, Mrs Fannie Rowan Young of 1030 Buena Vista Street, South Pasadena.

Lieutenant Young wrote his mother that the first he knew of the award [was] from British newspapers. The flyer is now training other young men to operate bombing planes.

His mother said she noticed more and more in his letters the spirit of sacrifice of the young flyer. He places no value on his own life other than how it can help his country.

Notes
1. H.M. Young to Father Sill, 18 March 1940.
2. Letter, Cheshire to Alan Cooper, 27 April 1981, courtesy Ian Sayer.
3. From Hullavington,18 March 1940.
4. Hullavington, 18 March 1940.
5. *Good and Faithful Servants*, Galloway and Rawll.
6. Ref. Pitkin Guide 1990.
7. Columbia Encyclopedia.
8. Hullavington, 18 March 1940.
9. *No Passing Glory*, Andrew Boyle.
10. Letter from H.M.Young to Father Sill, 16 May 1940.
11. Roosevelt did indeed set the US aircraft industry a production target of 50,000 warplanes a year in this message.
12. One of White's photographs shows Melvin using a paddle as they get near the ship.
13. One of White's photographs shows this heroic deed by the sailor – there is no record of him receiving the medal he deserved.
14. Actually Belfast.
15. Sergeant Burns.
16. Pilot Officer Forsdyke.
17. Ref. *RAF Coastal Command 1936-1969*, Chris Ashworth.
18. Letter from Clementine Rawson to Father Sill, January 1941.
19. Ref. RAF Record of Service.

Chapter 6

Instructing on Wellingtons

1941 was a critical period in the war and coincided with many movements for Melvin. He would, no doubt, have been granted some leave after his tour with 102 Squadron. The records of his postings enable us to get a feel for a fairly hectic period. Initially he was posted back to 10 OTU at Abingdon as an instructor on his familiar Whitley aircraft; his RAF Record of Service has two posting dates, 7 March for a Flying Officer post and 17 March as a Flight Lieutenant (his acting rank).[1] Whatever the exact date of arrival, he spent approximately one month at Abingdon and it can be assumed that he spent the time 'learning the ropes' as an instructor.

The 10 OTU records show that on 17 March 1941 the first course arrived, consisting entirely of Empire Air Training Scheme trainees; men who had received their flying training thus far in Canada, South Africa and other parts of the British Empire. Also on that day A.J.P. Taylor, Fellow of Magdalen College Oxford, lectured at 19.00 on 'NAZI GERMANY'. Taylor, who in later years became famous for his many books and television lectures, returned on 23 March to give a talk, 'WHAT HAPPENED TO FRANCE'. Melvin might well have attended these talks.

In between the training activities at Abingdon, there were reminders of the realities of war. On 18 March seven Wellingtons had to land at Abingdon on return from a raid on Bremen.

On 21 March enemy aircraft dropped twenty-nine bombs; twenty-eight falling outside the base, but one damaged the building housing the headquarters of 6 Group and killed one person. On the same day Air Marshal A.G.R. Garrod, the Air Member for Training, had visited the station. Alfred Guy Roland Garrod MC, had commanded 13 Squadron and its RE8s in France at the end of the First World War. The author's uncle, Second Lieutenant C.C.A. Daniel, was one of the 13 Squadron pilots at that time. On a practical level, Angle of Glide Indicators were put into use at Abingdon and its satellite, Stanton Harcourt, on 12 April.

As a principal training base RAF Abingdon saw a number of events and VIP visitors. On 23 March the King had ordered a Day of National Prayer, so there was a parade and service at 09.30, and later the RAF Central Orchestra gave a concert. On 7 April the Deputy Inspector General of the Polish Air Force, Group Captain Iwasczkiewicz, visited and inspected Polish personnel. On 15 April the Right Honourable Sir Archibald Sinclair, the Secretary of State for Air flew in to Abingdon at 17.35, saw some of the ground training in progress and a Whitley V aircraft, and left again, by air, at 18.40. Then on 17 April, the first officer of the United States Army Air Corps arrived. Although the USA was not yet in the war, it was a precursor of greater things to come.

Then, on 19 April, now fully promoted to Flight Lieutenant, Melvin was sent to No. 21 OTU at Moreton-in-Marsh for a conversion course on the Vickers Wellington bomber. The Wellington, from the famous Vickers' stable at Weybridge, had been designed as a medium bomber to the 1932 specification B9/32. It was to prove one of the most versatile aircraft to enter RAF service, and 11,391 Wellingtons of numerous marks were to be built during the war. It was sturdy and reliable, being of a unique geodetic metal lattice construction, and was designed by Dr Barnes Wallis, who had also been the designer of the successful R.100 airship.

The Wellington is described in Hugh Bergel's book *Flying Wartime Aircraft* from the perspective of the Air Transport Auxiliary (ATA) ferry pilots:

The Wellington, known as the 'Wimpy', was universally loved. It was the first big aeroplane flown by ATA pilots who had converted to Class IV[2] on the Blenheim, but it was such a docile and friendly thing that this worried nobody. Because, I suppose, its unique geodetic construction was more flexible than the normal all-metal construction, it had the habit – not in the least disconcerting – of twitching slightly from time to time as it rattled along; it was almost as if it was wagging its tail at you. It was very easy to fly (though a bit marginal if one engine failed), and the view from the cockpit was good enough to make it one of the better aeroplanes for bad weather flying. And it was exceptionally easy to land.

The official *Pilot's Notes for the Wellington (A.P. 1578)* include checklists which are not much different from those of most light aircraft. This handbook states that the aircraft is directionally and longitudinally stable, with only slight stability on the climb. Laterally, depressing a wing causes the nose to drop, with slow recovery of the wing. Regarding the effect of the controls it says that when flying in bumpy weather, pilots may experience a slight 'kick' on the controls, originating from the elevator and rudder.[3] This does not interfere in any way with the control of the aircraft and can be ignored.

Melvin was at 21 OTU only from 19-25 April, long enough to convert onto the Wellington, even though the flying programme had been curtailed due to bad weather and aircraft unserviceability from 15-20th. During April 1941 21 OTU received nine Wellington Ic aircraft, operationally equipped; two Avro Ansons and two Wellington Ics for instructional purposes. This made a total strength of twenty-five operational and two instructional Wellingtons and six Ansons. The Wellington Mark I was powered by two Bristol Pegasus XVIII air cooled, radial engines of 1,050hp each. The Mark II, which Melvin was to operate in 104 Squadron, was equipped with Rolls-Royce Merlin X water cooled engines of 1,145hp each. Other marks of Wellington were fitted with somewhat more powerful Bristol Hercules or Pratt & Whitney engines.

21 OTU had its share of excitement at the time. On the night of 25/26 April six men had to parachute, over Breconshire, from an Anson, captained by Pilot Officer Wetherby. Fortunately they

received only minor injuries although the aircraft was destroyed. On 30 April three Wellingtons made forced landings at Windrush, Dybury and Abingdon.

Melvin was next destined for the newly formed 22 OTU, equipped with Wellington aircraft, at the equally new aerodrome at Wellesbourne Mountford, four miles east of Stratford-upon-Avon and very close to the Tudor mansion Charlecote Park, where Shakespeare is reputed to have done a bit of youthful poaching. The Operations Record Book for 22 OTU shows Wing Commander L.G. Harman, DFC, as the Chief Flying Instructor as of 14 April 1941. One of the first movements recorded at Wellesbourne Mountford was on 15 April, when Lieutenant (Miss) Anna Leska, Polish Air Force, of No. 3 Ferry Pilots School landed a Miles Magister due to poor visibility on the way to Stroud. Lieutenant Lenska was one of the Poles who escaped the Germans by 'borrowing' an aircraft and flying it to exile. She continued on her way the next day, and served with the ATA (later as Mrs Anna Daab) until the organization was disbanded on 30 November 1945.

The 22 OTU ORB shows Melvin arriving at Wellesbourne on 25 April 1941, from 10 OTU, 'on posting for flying duties' with no mention of 21 OTU. His Record of Service shows him posted to 22 OTU on 30 April, 'Screened Instructor Duties'.

Wartime OTUs were necessarily very busy. During Melvin's time at Wellesbourne, April to August 1941, six courses started. Pilots, air observers (navigators), wireless operators/air gunners and air gunners were all trained. Flying training, both day and night is recorded as starting on 8 May, coinciding with the first attack on the aerodrome by the Luftwaffe, when eleven bombs were dropped at 01.00, causing slight damage to the fire tender building. The enemy seemed determined to disrupt the OTU; they attacked again at 01.10 on the 10th, causing slight damage to a Wellington, and again on the 12th, dropping twelve bombs at 00.58 when two Wellingtons and an Anson were rendered unserviceable.

The high level of flying activity led to the opening of a satellite (overflow) aerodrome, known as Stratford, at Atherstone-on-Stour, on 5 July 1941, and 'B' Flight of 22 OTU moved there on

12 July. This aerodrome was located in line with the main south-westerly runway at Wellesbourne, so careful coordination was necessary. At one point thirty-two Wellingtons and three Ansons were recorded as being on strength although at any one time as many as half could be unserviceable.

The ORB records that rapid strides were made by the Navigation Section, and before his next posting, to 104 Squadron on 2 September, Melvin is recorded as 'Navigation Officer'. The cross-country flights by 'C' Flight (the navigation flight) were re-organized. The majority of night trips used Fishguard, on the south-west tip of Wales, as a turning point, 'to enable infra-red photo exercises to be carried out'. It was notable that the marking of all balloon barrages on all air maps came into force in July – presumably there had been too many accidents and close-calls with balloon cables.

The new base at Wellesbourne received a good share of important visitors during Melvin's time there. On 26 May the Air Officer Commanding came and flew with pupils of No. 1 Course. On 23 July the Right Honourable Mr P. Fraser, Prime Minister of New Zealand, visited and gave a talk to the New Zealand contingent on the base. This occasion was chosen for the dedication of the Camp Chapel by the Bishop of Coventry, whose own cathedral had been so notably destroyed in the infamous Luftwaffe raid of 14 November 1940, when the enemy had made good use of their radio navigation aids. Such benefits were yet to come for the RAF. Air Marshal Garrod, the Air Member for Training, extended his visits to OTUs to Wellesbourne, flying in on 3 August.

The hazards of flying were considerable during the Second World War. This applied to the training sphere as well as to operations. It was a time of rapid development in aircraft when the performance of the aircraft was sometimes in advance of the training and experience of the crews, and the technology was rapidly becoming more complex. There was great pressure to produce crews for operations and inevitably risks were accepted which would have been avoided in peacetime. Maintenance technicians also worked under time pressure, and often in unfavourable conditions in the open. The British weather is seldom good for long. All these factors meant that a significant proportion of casualties occurred during training.

On 26 June, Wellington R1586 of 22 OTU crashed at Loxley, two miles to the south-west of the aerodrome, and its crew of five were killed. There were other less serious accidents; Wellington (Mk1c) R1782 suffered a starboard undercarriage collapse on 1 September, the crew being uninjured. The ORB also records accidents in the area to aircraft from other bases:

A Hampden bomber of 106 Squadron from Coningsby crashed at nearby Hampton Lucy on 27 May; the pilot was killed and the three others were injured.

On 6 August a Whitley of 77 Squadron from Topcliffe crashed half a mile south of Alveston and all the crew were killed.

On the wider war front, momentous events were unfolding. The Germans had invaded Yugoslavia and Greece, using their superior air power to great effect. This air power was demonstrated most notably in the Battle of Crete, when the island was captured by airborne forces. The Royal Navy suffered heavy losses in the seas around that island. Simultaneously the epic chase and destruction of the battleship *Bismarck* was taking place in the stormy north Atlantic, at the cost to the Royal Navy of its most famous ship, the elegant but elderly battlecruiser HMS *Hood*. Melvin must have been concerned for his naval contemporaries such as Con Cherry. Then on 22 June came Operation Barbarossa, the German invasion of the Soviet Union, starting four years of the most bitter fighting on land.

Melvin had mixed feelings about his time teaching new aircrew, but he undoubtedly applied himself to the task with his usual thoroughness and determination. It is not clear how much time, if any, was available for recreation; it is likely that he revisited Stratford, but under less relaxed circumstances than during his visit with his school friends, Ed Rawson and Dudley Johnson, only six years previously. Indeed, Melvin wrote to Father Sill from Wellesbourne Mountford[4] saying that he was near Stratford-upon-Avon 'in some of the loveliest country in England'. He wrote:

I sadly missed operational flying but everybody has to have periods of rest while they teach others and I don't suppose I have a hope of getting back before the fall and I shall be lucky if I do then, God willing and I survive the hazards of being flown around by pilots under training.

Also in his letter, he commiserated with Father Sill who had been forced to retire as headmaster of Kent School because of his health and wished him well. Melvin wrote:

I feel now that you will be happy in your well deserved rest, knowing that your life's work is continuing as you made it. To look at Kent is to remember her first Headmaster and I am reminded of the famous epitaph on Wren's plain stone tombstone in St Paul's – "Si monumentum requiris, circumspice".

He added a handwritten footnote to this typed letter:

I am very pleased to be able to tell you that I think I am the first Kent man with a DFC which I was given a few days ago.

At about this time he and his father made a joint present of a silver tankard to Trinity College[5] and Melvin found time to take it to Oxford personally, as recorded by a letter of thanks, dated 9 June 1941, from Philip Landon to Henry Young. Landon commented that: 'Melvin always seems very cheerful and happy, and we were all very glad when he got his DFC.' Melvin would also have been saddened to learn of the damage that had been suffered by Westminster School due to German air raids on London, which continued despite the Luftwaffe being occupied further east. On the night of 10/11 May Westminster School's great hall, known as School, and part of the dormitory of the eleventh century monastery, was destroyed by fire, as was the College Dormitory, designed by Sir Christopher Wren. The Busby Library had received a direct hit during a previous raid. The school was in distinguished company that night as the nearby Chamber of the House of Commons was also destroyed by fire.

Nonetheless, Melvin's experience was needed for operations

and so on 2 September, after a little over four months in Warwickshire, he left Wellesbourne and, on the 4th, arrived at Driffield in Yorkshire, this time to join 104 Squadron, for flying duties as a Squadron Leader, which acting rank he assumed on 7 September. 104 Squadron has as its motto 'STRIKE HARD' and the crest shows a winged baton with flaming ends, surrounded by lightning strikes.[6]

Notes
1. The Air Historical Branch (AHB) records the 17 March date.
2. Larger twin- engined aircraft.
3. cf. Bergel's twitching.
4. Letter dated 11 May 1941 from H.M. Young to Father Sill.
5. Trinity College Report, 1940/1.
6. Author's description, with apologies to the College of Heralds.

Chapter 7

Wellingtons in Malta and Egypt

Melvin's move to 104 Squadron not only took him back to Driffield, but put him under the command of Wing Commander P.R. Beare, with whom he had served in 102 Squadron. Philip Robert Beare, who went on to become a Group Captain and remained in the RAF for many years after the war, was extremely popular among his colleagues, both junior and senior, being known as 'Teddy Bear' or 'Maxie'. A Cornishman, born in 1914, and educated at The King's School, Peterborough, he joined the RAF in 1935 and trained at Brough on the edge of the Humber, flying the Blackburn B2, and in Shropshire.

Philip Beare had been posted to command 104 Squadron on 8 May 1941. Of modest height (5 feet 6 inches) with brown hair and grey eyes, he was of sturdy build and was famous for his handlebar moustache. He was featured in a book *Drawing the RAF*, in which there is an impressive profile of him wearing a fleece lined jacket and leather flying helmet. The artist was the famous Eric Kennington, whose portrait of Melvin's Trinity rowing colleague, Richard Hillary, resides in the National Portrait Gallery.

Melvin's first flight of his second tour was a 'nursery' raid, attacking the docks at Boulogne – it was considered sensible to get re-accustomed to battle with a relatively simple operation. The aircraft was Wellington Z8400, EP-A, and the crew were Acting Squadron Leader Young (pilot), Sergeant Richardson (co-pilot), Pilot Officer Fairbairn (observer), Sergeant Bartley (No. 1 wireless operator), Sergeant Franks (No. 2 wireless operator) and Sergeant Redler (air gunner). They were airborne at 18.32 and landed back at Driffield at 23.30. The ORB shows that they attacked at 21.25 from 5,500 feet with 6/10ths cloud at 4,000 feet, dropping a mixed load of 250, 500 and 1,000lb bombs. Bursts were seen between docks 4, 6 and 7 and several fires were started.

Melvin's second period at Driffield was short, because an element of fifteen crews and aircraft from 104 Squadron was detached to join 238 Wing of 205 Group of the Middle East Air Force. Thus, on 14 October an advance party, under Melvin's command, moved to Stanton Harcourt, a satellite aerodrome for Abingdon. A few days later he left for Malta in Wellington Z8414, arriving there without incident, at Luqa aerodrome, on 20 October in company with aircraft piloted by Pilot Officers Ferry, Grey and Goodwin and Sergeants Forster, Bennett and Knights. Philip Beare had preceded Melvin to Malta by two days, accompanied by five aircraft; two other aircraft had flown to Malta via Portreath (Cornwall) and Gibraltar, also arriving on 18 October.

Malta has been described as 'The Key to Africa'. With the British engaged in a desperate battle to keep the Axis forces from invading Egypt and then the oilfields of the Middle East, Malta was crucial to both sides. If the British held it they could, and did, disrupt the flow of men and supplies to the Germans and Italians in North Africa. Had the island fallen the situation in the Mediterranean would have become impossible. Thus air and sea battles raged around Malta from mid 1940, when Italy entered the war, until 1943 when the Axis had finally been defeated in Africa and Sicily was invaded.

The story of the Second Siege of Malta is well documented elsewhere; the first was a gory affair between the Knights Hospitallers and the Turks in 1565. Suffice it to say that the George Cross awarded to the people of Malta by King George VI in April 1942 was hard earned.

The Wellington bombers were based at Luqa, an established aerodrome with runways, and its satellite 'Safi Strip', the two being connected by a tortuous series of taxiways, off which were located numerous dispersal sites for parked aircraft, and which

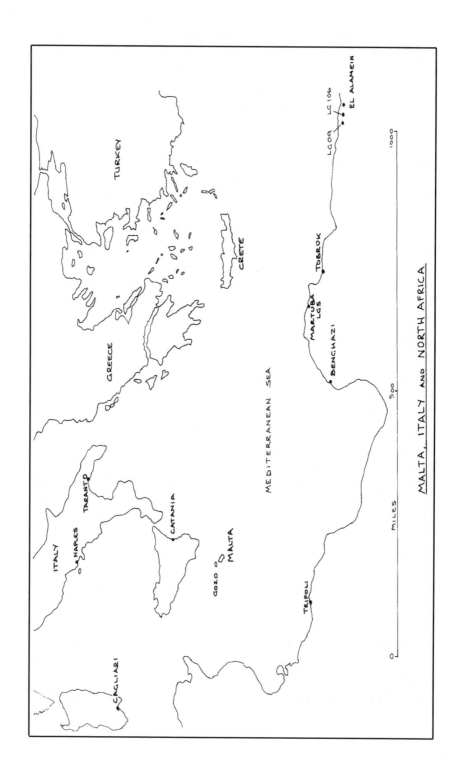

MALTA, ITALY AND NORTH AFRICA

continued southwards to another airfield, Hal Far. The dispersals were given some protection by blast walls (revetments) made of local stone or sand filled petrol cans – hard work for local labourers and British soldiers; it could take 60,000 cans to build a blast pen. The filling in of bomb craters added to the effort required. There were a few heavy rollers but much work was done by hand. Some days there were as many as 3,000 infantry and Royal Artillery troops at work. Each airfield was more or less adopted by a brigade. Famous county regiments became associated with the various airfields. The Royal West Kents and the Buffs were at Luqa, the Manchesters at Takali and the Devons at Hal Far but a feature of the organization was its flexibility, which enabled rush jobs of crater filling to be done by day or by night. Altogether some twenty-seven miles of dispersal tracks and hundreds of aircraft pens were constructed.

The airfields on Malta were subject to concentrated bombing attacks and many aircraft were lost on the ground as well as to intruding enemy fighters. The British air defence of Malta, by radar, guns and fighters was heroic. It was essential to be able to maintain the pressure on the Axis by our bombers and naval forces. The Wellington force was needed to attack the ends of the enemy supply lines, at Naples and Tripoli, although they ranged widely from Sicily to Greece, attacking shipping, harbour installations, airfields and factories.

In the autumn of 1941 the air onslaught on Malta was mainly by the Italians, the Luftwaffe being heavily committed on the Eastern Front, where Moscow was within fifteen miles of being overrun but, ominously for 1942, the Luftwaffe started returning to Sicily in December 1941 with the intention of finishing Malta as a threat to the Axis. It was a posting of some hardship as supplies had to come by sea at great risk of attack, whether via Gibraltar in the west or Alexandria to the east. When Melvin returned to Malta in May 1942 for the second time the air battle was at its most intense. The German Commander-in-Chief South of the Axis Forces, Kesselring, was determined '...to safeguard our supply lines by smoking out that hornet's nest'. Thus Malta has been described as the most bombed place on earth.

To keep the pressure on the British in the Mediterranean, and thus on Malta, in late 1941 Hitler moved half of his Atlantic submarine force through the Straits of Gibraltar. This resulted in more heavy losses for the Royal Navy. In November 1941 the aircraft carrier HMS *Ark Royal* was torpedoed by *U-81* and sank near Gibraltar and the battleship *Barham* was hit by a salvo of torpedoes from *U-331* in the eastern Mediterranean, suffering a magazine explosion and heavy loss of life. The naval situation was made worse by the disabling of the battleships *Valiant* and *Queen Elizabeth* in Alexandria harbour by Italian 'human torpedoes' which was a retaliation for the famous Royal Navy air strike on Taranto a year earlier. In December even worse news came from the Far East when a force of Japanese aircraft sank the new battleship *Prince of Wales* and the old battlecruiser *Repulse* off Malaya.

It is an interesting comparison to see that Melvin's great rowing friend Conrad Cherry, now a Lieutenant in the Royal Naval Volunteer Reserve had a part in the epic that was the Siege of Malta. Con Cherry was serving on the fast minelayer HMS *Welshman*, a ship of 4,000 tons but fitted with engines as powerful as a cruiser of twice the displacement. It was thus capable of very high speeds (up to forty knots for limited periods) and was used to carry urgent supplies into Malta, running through the areas most exposed to air attack in the hours of darkness. It is unlikely that Con and Melvin would have met in Malta; *Welshman's* visits were short and sharp. One of the ship's most famous dawn arrivals was on 10 May 1942 at 05.25, at the height of the Luftwaffe's attacks, when she was loaded with ammunition for the anti-aircraft guns. The bombs started raining down soon after through a smokescreen, as sailors and soldiers hurriedly unloaded the ship. *Welshman* sailed again that evening. Sadly she ran the gauntlet once too often and was eventually torpedoed by *U-617* between Crete and Tobruk on 1 February 1943, sinking with heavy loss of life, including Con Cherry.

In keeping with the strategic situation it was a time of considerable air activity in Malta when 104 Squadron arrived. On the night after his arrival, 21 October 1941, Melvin led a force of

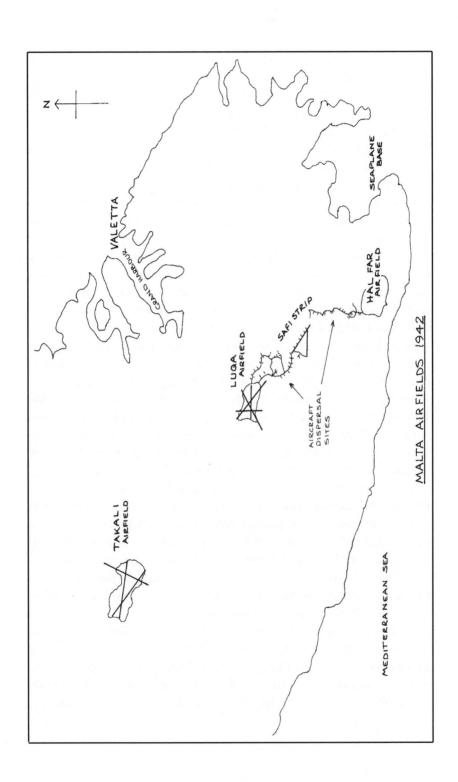

MALTA AIRFIELDS 1942

thirteen aircraft from 104 Squadron, accompanied by twelve from 38 Squadron, to attack Naples. Melvin and his crew were in their usual aircraft, A for Apple, dropping 8,500lb bombs in two sticks, and unloaded some incendiaries in Sicily en route and starting fires there. On 24 October six Wellingtons, led by Philip Beare and Melvin, attacked Tripoli. Tripoli was again the target on the 29th, with twelve aircraft attacking the marshalling yards to disrupt enemy supplies. Melvin's aircraft bombed the target but could not see the results as they were caught in the beams of searchlights. Melvin's October operations ended on the 31st with a raid by nine aircraft on an aircraft factory at Naples, which is still a main centre for the aeronautical industry in Italy. His crew dropped a single 4,000lb bomb, but no results were seen and the bomb was suspected to have been a 'dud', failing to explode. On the other hand, the Italian searchlights and anti-aircraft fire were ineffective. At this time Philip Beare was awarded the DSO, the citation included a mention of a daylight raid on Brest on 24 July 1941. He was to be awarded a Bar to the DSO in May 1943 while serving with 70 Squadron.

November continued with the same high level of activity for 104 Squadron, sometimes raiding north to Italy, sometimes south to Libya. On 2 November, Philip Beare led ten aircraft to Castel Benito aerodrome south of Tripoli. Melvin and his crew claimed a direct hit on a two-engined aircraft which 'disintegrated'. On the 5th, a good night for fireworks, ten aircraft raided the aerodromes at Mellaha and Castel Benito. On Armistice Day, 11 November, nine aircraft, including Melvin's, raided Naples. He then had a brief pause from operations until the 20th, when he led three aircraft on a 'nuisance raid' on Brindisi. Melvin, in A for Apple as usual, stayed over the target for two hours, dropping high explosive and incendiary bombs, singly and from various heights between 9,000 and 11,000 feet, starting some fires. On the 27th, Philip Beare led Melvin and another seven aircraft to the Royal Arsenal at Naples. This was described as a very successful raid, hitting a torpedo factory, aircraft works, oil tanks and a railway station. To finish November in a geographically even-handed way, ten aircraft,

The Oxford Crew practise for the 1938 Boat Race. Melvin far left of picture.

Informal photograph of 1938 Oxford Eight, in 'Boat Order'. Melvin (No.2), second from left.

The Oxford Eight preparing for the 1938 Boat Race at Putney.

The winning Oxford Boat Race crew, 1938. Melvin second from left, back row;
Conrad Cherry holding trophy.

Melvin's oar used in the 1938 Boat Race. (Photo. David Young)

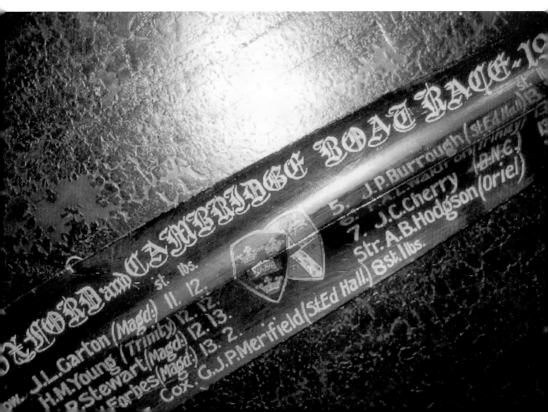

OXFORD and CAMBRIDGE BOAT RACE·19

5. J.P.Burrough (St Ed Hall)

7. J.C.Cherry (B.N.C.)

Str. A.B.Hodgson (Oriel)

st. lbs.

J.L.Garton (Magd:) 11. 12.

H.M.Young (Trinity) 12. 12.

Stewart (Magd:) 12. 13.

Forbes (Magd:) 13. 2.

Cox. G.J.P.Merifield (St Ed Hall) 8 st. lbs.

A crew of Oxford students, including Melvin Young, racing in Germany in 1938, probably at Bad Ems.

Oxford oarsmen relax in Germany - Melvin partly hidden at rear.

115/117 Fore St., Hertford - Henry Young had his office and flat here - Melvin sometimes gave it as his address. (Author 2004)

Rev. Arthur Harrington 'Bill' Franklin, sometime teacher at Kent and Westminster Schools and friend of Melvin Young.

Alan Tyser, a rowing friend tutored by Melvin Young before entering Trinity College - Melvin took him for a ride in a Lancaster. (Trinity College, Oxford)

End of course dinner menu, No. 9 Service Flying Training School, Hullavington, 2 April 1940. Cartoons: Melvin Young sitting cross legged, Leonard Cheshire entering pawn brokers.

Signatures on the reverse of Melvin's copy of the end of course dinner menu.

102 Squadron 1940. Melvin Young back row, far right; Leonard Cheshire middle row, second from left; Philip Beare front row, fourth from left.

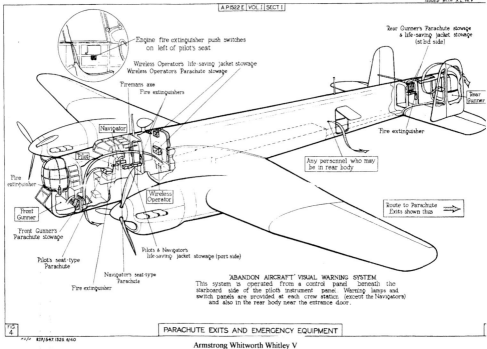

A.P.1522 E | VOL.1 | SECT I

Engine fire extinguisher push switches
on left of pilot's seat

Wireless Operators life-saving jacket stowage
Wireless Operators Parachute stowage

Firemans axe
Fire extinguishers

Navigator

Pilot

Fire
extinguisher

Front
Gunner

Front Gunner's
Parachute stowage

Wireless
Operator

Pilot's seat-type
Parachute

Navigator's seat-type
Parachute

Fire extinguisher

Pilots & Navigators
life-saving jacket stowage (port side)

Rear Gunner's Parachute stowage
& life-saving jacket stowage
(st bd side)

Rear
Gunner

Fire extinguisher

Any personnel who may
be in rear body

Route to Parachute
Exits shown thus ⟶

'ABANDON AIRCRAFT' VISUAL WARNING SYSTEM.
This system is operated from a control panel beneath the
starboard side of the pilots instrument panel. Warning lamps and
switch panels are provided at each crew station (except the Navigators)
and also in the rear body near the entrance door.

FIG 4

R.T.P./547.1325. 6/40

PARACHUTE EXITS AND EMERGENCY EQUIPMENT

Armstrong Whitworth Whitley V

Diagram of Whitley V, showing exits and emergency equipment.

Fannie Young and her sister Florence (in hat) at the ranch 'Cielito Lindo', September 1940.

Melvin and his crew in dinghy, 8 October 1940, from HMS St *Mary's*. Another
escort vessel stands by.

Dinghy alongside HMS St *Mary's*, Melvin holding line.

P/O Forsdyke (Observer) falls in the sea and is rescued by an heroic sailor.

Melvin discusses the rescue with Sgt Burns, rear gunner.

Melvin on HMS *St Mary's* with Lt Phibbs, the Captain.

Rescue smile. Taken on HMS *St Mary's*, 8 October 1940. This was to become his family's favourite photograph of Melvin.

Wellesbourne Mountford Aerodrome, 2006. An industrial estate and modern housing occupy the wartime technical and accommodation areas. (Author 2006)

Silver tankard presented to Trinity College, Oxford, 1941, by Melvin Young and his father. (Trinity College)

104 Squadron, Rolls-Royce Merlin Engined Wellington II, Egypt 1942. W/Cdr Philip Beare, centre, with Melvin Young on his right and S/Ldr Brown on his left.

Egypt 1942. Melvin Young with W/Cdr Philip Beare, a Group Captain and a
Flight Lieutenant (possibly Intelligence Officer).

Melvin's British Forces
ID card, Egypt, March
1942. Height 6ft 1in,
Eyes Blue, Hair Brown.
Note the moustache
and determined
expression.

Passport photo, 1942, shortly before departure for USA. Now clean shaven and notably more relaxed.

Ravenscroft Farm, Skiff Mountain, near Kent, Connecticut. (Author 2005)

Kent School Chapel.
(Author 2005)

Wedding photograph,
Ravenscroft, 10 August
1942. Clementine
('Kempchen') Rawson,
Melvin, Priscilla and
Hobart Rawson.

including Melvin's, attacked administration buildings in Benghazi on the 29th.

It is notable from the 104 Squadron Record Book that during November Melvin started signing the 'Summary of Events' on behalf of Philip Beare. He also performed much routine flying; air tests on aircraft after maintenance, 'local' flying, including instructing second pilots, and searchlight cooperation.

On 5 December, ten 104 Squadron aircraft, including Melvin's, were back at the Royal Arsenal in Naples, but this time the antiaircraft fire was accurate. Two days later, with six other Wellingtons he set out for a fuel depot near Tripoli, but cloud obscured the target and they had to bomb targets of opportunity. Melvin did four more operations in 1941; a strike on shipping at Patros, minelaying at Tripoli and aerodrome raids at Castel Benito and Misurata. In this period came the stunning news of the Japanese attack on Pearl Harbor with the result that the USA entered the war. From his earlier correspondence with Father Sill, we know that Melvin felt that the active involvement of the USA would make all the difference, as it did, eventually. Despite all this activity Melvin found time to write to his sister Angela telling her about the history of Malta, but not about the operations in which he was engaged.

How they spent the Christmas of 1941 is not recorded but from his comments the following year we know it was in Malta, and no doubt the officers served dinner to the men, probably with unseasonably meagre rations. Then at the beginning of January 1942 the whole squadron moved to Kabrit in Egypt as part of 205 Group which operated night bombers in the Middle East and Mediterranean theatres of war, in readiness for the next onslaught by Rommel and his Afrika Korps. The war in the Western Desert, along the coast of North Africa, west of Egypt, had many changes of fortune, but 1942 was particularly dangerous to the Allies until the Battle of El Alamein in the autumn eventually turned the tide for good against the Axis. While all this was going on, the war raged elsewhere. A series of disasters for the Allies in the Far East was only brought to an end with the Battle of Midway on 4 June and, back in Britain, Bomber Command was at last starting to make itself truly felt in Germany, with the famous 1,000 bomber raid on Cologne on 30 May.

The author is indebted to F.R. Chappell who, in his book

Wellington Wings, gives us a first-hand account of the operations by 104 Squadron at this time[1]

Frances Roy Chappell was a school teacher in Dorset in peacetime, having studied geography at both Cambridge and London Universities, and in later life had a distinguished teaching career in Australia. In January 1942, at the age of thirty-two, he found himself as a very junior Acting Pilot Officer serving as Squadron Intelligence Officer with 104 Squadron. He was acutely aware that he was briefing aircrew who, although generally younger and less mature than he was, were much more experienced in the practicalities and hazards of operating bombers.

Chappell describes 205 Group as:

> ...a smaller Bomber Command...a tightly organised and efficient bombing force, flexible enough to be switched in emergency to direct army support in attacking enemy tanks, transport and troops close to the front line. Operating conditions for the men of these night bomber squadrons were very different from the conditions prevailing for Bomber Command crews in Europe. The 205 Group Squadrons were units of a mobile bomber force based in tents, trucks and improvised runways scraped from the desert surface...airfield equipment was primitive, maintenance of engines and airframes difficult, living conditions always uncomfortable, 'gippy tummy' was common, relaxation in cities with music, dancing and female company was rare indeed; rising sand and *Khamsin* conditions[2], hot humid days and freezing nights were part of the environment...on the happier side, weather conditions were settled for longer periods and targets were usually less heavily defended than in Germany and losses on normal missions were lower than for Bomber Command. Exceptions were the 'Mail Run', regular targets frequently attacked, such as Benghazi and Tobruk.

Another insight into the Wellington operations is found in *RAF Middle East, The Official Story of Air Operations in the Middle East, from February 1942 to January 1943*. It is worth quoting:

Sometimes they struck northwards over the Mediterranean at targets in Greece and Crete, but their chief task...was to batter Benghazi. They did this raid so often in a climate where bad weather rarely interferes with night flying that they nicknamed it the 'mail run'. Yet it was no easy flight. In distance it was roughly the equivalent of bombing Munich from Norfolk.[3] The route was not splattered with guns and searchlights, but on the other hand a crew had to crash-land only 50 miles inland on the desert to be faced with the torments, often mortal, of thirst and heat. And the defences of Benghazi itself were fierce...

The mail run to Benghazi was made on 23 nights in March (1942), 24 in April and 21 in May...

Night after night the Wellingtons throbbed through the searchlights and AA fire, the bomb-aimers crouched on their stomachs against the Perspex in the nose, the pilots turning this way and that in evasive action, the gunners searching the bright moonlight for night fighters. From above, the harbour looks almost too insignificant for all that trouble. The moles and the inner harbour form a rough box-shape with the Cathedral mole sticking down in the centre. It is quite easy under an African moon to discern detail, even the little projections nicknamed George, Harry and Johnny, which once were ships with such names as *Maria Eugenia* and *Gloriastella*, and now as wrecks filled with concrete, had become the main unloading piers...

Night after night it happened until at mid-summer...there was scarcely a building that had not suffered to some extent, that beside the wrecks in the harbour the outer mole had been broken in three places, that some half of the warehouses had been so damaged that great piles of stores stood in the open, that the powerhouse was silent, the railway sidings littered with bent and twisted rails. But ships were still coming into the harbour...supplies were still filtering through to the enemy armies in the desert...

Truly the Wellington force was engaged in a long hard battle.

Chappell describes his journey to join 104 Squadron in January 1942, on a bright but cool sunny day typical of the

Egyptian winter. He travelled in an RAF truck, from 205 Group HQ at Shallufa, in the Canal Zone, at the southern, Red Sea end, of the Suez Canal, to RAF Station Kabrit on the shore of the Great Bitter Lake:

> The road was bitumen – a dark line through a brown and grey expanse of sand and stony desert. To the right a line of green trees and irrigated fields marked the fresh water canal providing the only source of drinking water in the area and drawing its life giving fluid from the River Nile at Cairo some one hundred miles to the west. Beyond the fresh water canal and parallel to it was the Suez Ship Canal, here a straight stretch of twenty miles joining the Gulf of Suez to the Bitter Lakes – natural salt lakes in a depression of the desert surface.
>
> Near the Geneifa army camp with its huts, tents, training grounds, military cemetery, storage areas and motor transport parks, the RAF truck turned sharp right off the main Suez – Ismailia – Port Said road, crossed a railway and the Sweet Water Canal towards the blue expanse of water which was the southern part of the Great Bitter lake. The road turned northwards and followed the line of a concrete walled canal from Geneifa. In the distance appeared buildings and large hangars, a water tower, sand bagged dispersals and their encircled aircraft, recognisable as Wellington bombers by their tall fin protruding above the sand walls.

RAF Station Kabrit was the home base for two Wellington squadrons, 104 and 148. Chappell records that 104 Squadron had 'expected to return to Britain after their detachment to Malta. Instead, the surviving aircraft and crews were posted to the Middle East to reinforce the 205 Group force of night bombers.' They were formed into two flights, under Melvin and Squadron Leader D.J. Brown DFC, using additional new crews from 205 Group:

> Thus, the 'new' squadron at Kabrit included crews experienced in Bomber Command and Malta missions and others

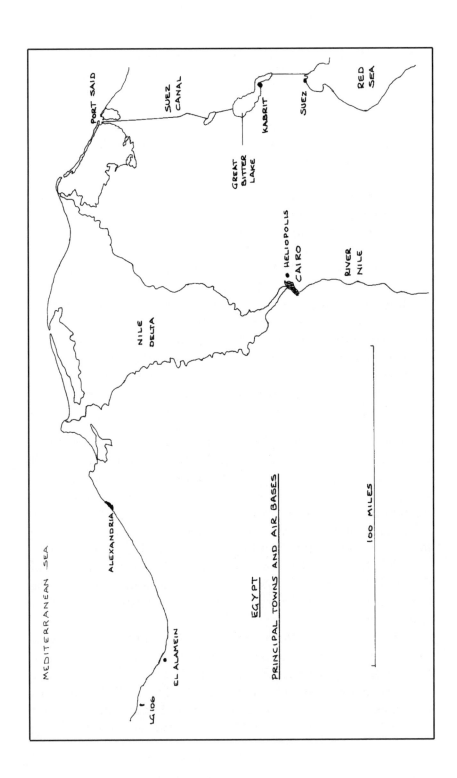

MEDITERRANEAN SEA

PORT SAID

SUEZ CANAL

GREAT BITTER LAKE

KABRIT

SUEZ

RED SEA

HELIOPOLIS

CAIRO

RIVER NILE

NILE DELTA

ALEXANDRIA

EL ALAMEIN

LG 106

EGYPT

PRINCIPAL TOWNS AND AIR BASES

100 MILES

starting their first tour of operations. As a squadron the crews were new to the conditions of desert warfare and some of the ex-Driffield types were not pleased to find themselves being regarded as 'new boys'. Even with the experienced leadership of Wing Commander Beare and Squadron Leader Young there was a feeling on the station that 104 had yet to establish themselves in the Middle East and the squadron personnel in February 1942 were sensitive about the matter. By contrast 148 were regarded by station administration and intelligence as an experienced and knowledgeable squadron under their extremely efficient and pleasant leader, Wing Commander J D Rollinson.

On 30 January 1942 RAF Station Kabrit was officially disbanded as such and reformed as No 236 Medium Bomber Wing operating Nos 104 and 148 Wellington Bomber Squadrons. The change meant little at the time but was in keeping with a plan to make wings and squadrons mobile, ready to move to advanced landing grounds in the Western Desert as and when moves in the front line made it necessary to operate bombers away from the permanent bases in the Canal Zone.

The high level direction of the war filtered down to 236 Wing in the form of instructions detailing the target, number of aircraft required, bomb load and type of bombs. Photo reconnaissance ascertained the state of the target area before and after each operation. The scale of operations was fairly high in February 1942 with Benghazi, which Rommel had recaptured on 29 January, enemy desert landing grounds such as the Martuba complex fifteen miles south of Derna, between Tobruk and Benghazi and airfields and ports in Crete and Greece as the main targets, with occasional shipping strikes against Axis supply convoys.

In order to increase the bomb load or range of the Wellingtons, use was made of Advanced Landing Grounds (ALGs) in the Daba area. In particular 236 Wing used LG 106, some twenty miles west of El Alamein, and sometimes LG09 (Bir Koraiyim) a few miles further west. The aircraft were bombed up at Kabrit and fuelled to reach Daba with a reserve to return if necessary.

At the ALG the aircraft were refuelled for the operation and the crews given last minute meteorological and intelligence briefings. On returning from the missions the aircraft landed at the ALG for an intelligence debriefing before flying back to Kabrit. Eventually it was decided to move the Wellington squadrons into the desert landing grounds and this happened in May for 104 Squadron.

Chappell makes several references to Melvin. He clearly had great respect for Melvin's record and leadership but sometimes was disturbed by his manner. Chappell records, on 13 March 1942 at ALG 106:

At the briefing by Squadron Leader Young he shut me out entirely. He is a large and formidable man with great experience and fame as a courageous bomber pilot but seems impatient with non-flying types such as IOs.[4] I can understand this.

However on 14 April his diary reads:

Another dust storm is brewing – commonly called here a 'shit-storm' – everything is 'shit' – flak is usually referred to by our aircrews as 'shit coming up'. Breathing was unpleasant at lunch time but the storm didn't reach *Khamsin* proportions. This evening I did the map build-up and briefing for the Martuba LGs. Four Wellingtons of 104 under the charge of Squadron Leader Young and the aircraft were afterwards going straight back to base. The Squadron Leader was more pleasant to me than usual – it must be the new Intelligence tent.

A few weeks later, on 3 May 1942, Chappell referred to an evening briefing for the 'mail run' to Benghazi and the Martuba landing grounds:

My briefing went quite well, in spite of Squadron Leader Young starting it by saying that no briefing was necessary. He's correct in some ways, of course, for most crews know Benghazi.

These comments by Chappell are among the few that describe Melvin as other than amiable. Melvin commented in a speech at Kent School how disagreeable he found the heat, sand and flies in Egypt and no doubt the conditions and the stresses of war made everyone tense.

On 23 May, Chappell records how he 'had a mad journey...to LG106 for a special briefing for my squadron which is sending a detachment of ten Wellingtons off to Malta under command of Squadron Leader H M Young. I'm glad to be back and listened to the briefing and watched the crews take-off with feeling.' At the end of the month he noted: 'Wing Commander P R (Teddy) Beare DFC left the squadron in May...with his hard-working flight commanders, Squadron Leader Young and Squadron Leader Brown, the efficient and cheerful Wing Commander had welded our squadron into an excellent and respected bomber unit of 205 Group'. He also described Melvin as 'selfless in his complete devotion to the task of bombing efficiently' – a recognition of the determined character which Melvin showed in so many fields, becoming good even if, as in his flying, he was not a 'natural'.

In addition to Chappell's invaluable diary, we can glean further information from other sources, including the 104 Squadron ORB. At one period, 6-16 April 1942, extra responsibility was placed on Melvin's shoulders as Philip Beare was away inspecting landing grounds in Palestine and Syria. On 14 April Melvin led three aircraft to attack the Martuba landing ground, dropping three sticks of bombs among the aircraft there. On 1 May, he took part in an attack on the Portolago Bay submarine base. In addition to operational flying there were instructional flights, circuits and landings with second pilots, air tests and searchlight cooperation. Philip Beare's logbook shows two flights with Melvin; on 22 March with Melvin as captain, 'Self very ill'; (possibly the strain was telling on Beare) and on 27 March, with Beare as captain, testing a new design of oil cooler which proved 'OK for oil but cuts down speed'. Photographs from this period show that Melvin had grown a neat moustache; perhaps as a Squadron Leader he wanted to look a bit older and on 1 June 1942 he received his substantive promotion to that rank. Notably, a few months later, at the time of his marriage, he was clean shaven again.

On 5 May 1942, Philip Beare was posted to Headquarters RAF Middle East and Wing Commander J. Blackburn DFC took over command of 104 Squadron. On 13 May the squadron moved forward to Landing Ground 106, by the coastal railway line twenty miles to the west of El Alamein, to reduce the transit times to enemy targets. However, on 23 May Melvin led a detachment of ten 104 Squadron Wellingtons, with twenty key maintenance personnel, five additional crews and certain heavy bombs, back to Malta for a period of intensive operations. Between 1-10 June they carried out eight operations against the Augusta Submarine base, Cagliari, Catania aerodrome, twice, Naples harbour and Taranto harbour, three times. This detachment resulted in a note, addressed to Air Commodore A.P. Ritchie AFC, AOC 205 Group, and passed on to Wing Commander Blackburn, from Air Marshal Tedder, the Commander-in-Chief, RAF Middle East:

> Please congratulate Squadron Leader Young of 104 Squadron on the excellent work done by him and his detachment of the squadron during the intensive operations at Malta. A first class effort.

Air Commodore Ritchie added, in his covering note, that:

> I have also received further details of the work of this detachment from the AOC, Malta, and it really was a splendid effort.

Melvin's tour with 104 Squadron resulted in him being gazetted, on 18 September 1942, for a Bar to his DFC. The citation reads:

Bar to Distinguished Flying Cross
  Squadron Leader Henry Melvin Young, DFC, RAFVR, No.104 Squadron
  This officer participated in the first large scale attack on Naples, pressing home his attack, in the face of an intense barrage, with great determination. On another occasion, he

bombed the Castel Benito aerodrome and then descended to 1,000 feet to machine gun dispersed aircraft by the light of flares released by other attacking aircraft. At least two aircraft on the ground were set on fire and a gun emplacement silenced.

On a further occasion, when returning to Malta from a raid on Tripoli, a stick of bombs burst on the aerodrome while Squadron Leader Young was landing his aircraft, setting fire to a bomb loaded aeroplane. Displaying great coolness, he completed his landing and avoided obstructions on the runway. He dispersed his aircraft, then took charge of the flare path and had it moved so that the remainder of the squadron were enabled to land safely. This officer has always shown the greatest courage and determination both in the air and on the ground. He has won the entire confidence of his crews.

In the RAF Museum Library there is a collection of papers left by Group Captain Philip Beare. Among them is a poignant, handwritten letter from Priscilla Young, written after Melvin's death from her family home in Connecticut. She congratulates Philip on the Bar to his DSO and says that Melvin had been:

> ...terribly pleased to get his DFC Bar last year and felt that he owed it entirely to your kind words. Melvin was apt to lack confidence in his own abilities and the only way in which he could gain assurance was to tackle some hard job. I feel the responsibility you gave him proved of invaluable help. I know he thought you let him take more responsibility than, as a Squadron Leader, he might otherwise have had.
>
> I could see that Melvin had grown up a great deal during his year in Egypt and I should like to say "thank you" for all the help you gave him.

Melvin now had a well-earned period of rest from operational flying. He had a brief period at HQ 205 Group at Bir El Gardabia where he was posted on 29 June and then, on 3 July, to 242 Wing, at Fayid, Egypt, for 'ferrying duties' with Liberators. Perhaps this was an administrative 'cover' for getting Melvin to America,

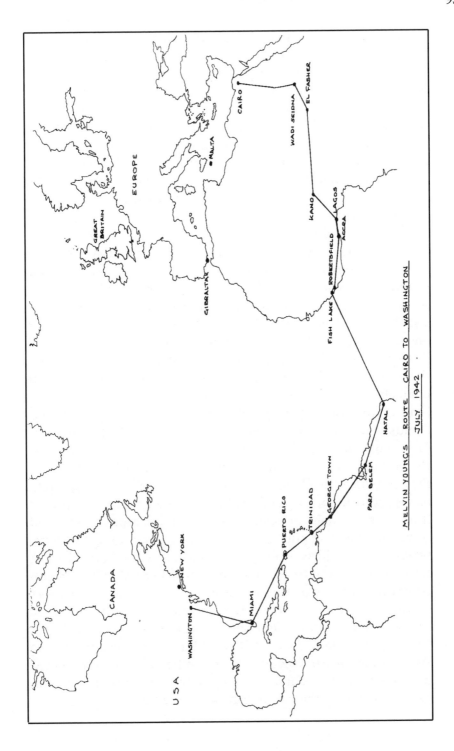

MELVIN YOUNG'S ROUTE CAIRO TO WASHINGTON
JULY 1942

where he was next posted to the RAF Delegation in Washington DC to take up temporary duties from 2 September with the United States Army Air Corps. Anyway, he was posted to No. 22 Personnel Transit Camp (PTC) Middle East on 17 July and on 24 July started a long, arduous journey to the USA. Melvin was travelling with Thomas Prickett, who had also been a flight commander on 148 Squadron flying Wellingtons in the Western desert, and who recorded the journey in his logbook – see Appendix 3. Tom Prickett recalled that the flights were in DC-3 aircraft operated by Pan American World Airways.[5]

This route was a well used ferry route for aircraft and personnel to and from Egypt and the USA, via West Africa and South America – the sector from Cairo to Kano had first been surveyed from the air in 1925 by Squadron Leader Arthur Coningham who was to be AOC of 4 Group when Melvin served with 102 Squadron. The flight set off southwards along the Nile from Heliopolis (Cairo) to Wadi Seidna, passing Luxor and the Valley of the Kings. The next day took them first to El Fasher in the Sudan, where there was 'a cool rest house built on the sand near the airfield with plain white rooms, scarlet blankets, and silent attentive Sudanese'[6] and then on to Kano, built of reddish clay and with an eleven mile city wall, and clouds of red dust around the airfield on the outskirts of the city. The two following days took them via Lagos and Accra to Robertsfield in Liberia and a short transfer to Fish Lake, where they embarked in a PanAm Clipper flying boat for an overnight eleven hour flight to Natal on the extreme eastern coastline of Brazil. The airfield at Natal was on sandy ground set amid scrub, but they had only a brief stop before continuing to Belem, where the airfield was also built on sand by the Para River. A flavour of the service provided by US airlines along the South American portion of this route is given in Ernest K. Gann's classic book *Fate is the Hunter*. Thereafter the flight proceeded for the next three days into English speaking territory via British Guiana, Trinidad, Puerto Rico, Miami and eventually to Washington DC. In a letter to his mother Melvin commented that he had taken eight days flying to the USA from Egypt and, having arrived at the end of July, was very tired.

Notes
1. This is particularly valuable because the 104 ORB for this period, at the National Archives, is so faint that it is difficult to read.
2. Fierce desert winds causing major dust storms.
3. Kabrit to Beghazi is c.700 miles.
4. Intelligence Officers.
5. Private correspondence with author.
6. *Atlantic Bridge*, HMSO, 1945.

Chapter 8

America and Marriage

Now began one of the most interesting periods of Melvin's life; certainly the most romantic. He arrived in the USA at the end of July 1942. On Saturday, 1 August, he telephoned his mother Fannie, in California, from New York City. He followed this with a short letter in which he told her that he had met some of the Rawsons (probably Ed and his father Hobart) and would be 'off to Kent at the crack of dawn to see the rest of the Rawson family and have a few days rest there and see the school again'. He had arranged to arrive at Kent shortly after breakfast and, being a great favourite with both Priscilla and her mother, he was to be made welcome. They had received a cable from Melvin on 23 July saying that he was 'Due in America the first week in August address the Air Attache, British Embassy Washington DC'. Melvin's RAF Record of Service shows that he was posted to the RAF Delegation, Washington, on temporary duty with the US Army Air Corps (USAAC).

His arrival at Ravenscroft Farm, on Sunday, 2 August, was indeed early in the morning. Before lunch, Melvin had proposed marriage to Priscilla. Although they had known each other for many years, were good friends, enjoyed each others company and conversation, and had spent time together in both the USA and England, this took Priscilla completely by surprise. She took a deep breath, and two days, before deciding to accept Melvin's proposal. Her brother, Ed, later remarked that 'Priscilla was always a good judge of character'. She had had other suitors, but had not taken any very seriously, and, at thirty-three years of age, seemed not to be looking for marriage, although when she telephoned her brother to say she was getting married his immediate question was 'Which one?'

Priscilla was a well-educated, well-travelled young woman, with a considerable knowledge of literature and music, but she was never much interested in matters of fashion or glamour. She was somewhat above average height, slim and rather short sighted. She had an independent income and no need of a husband to support her. Like Melvin, she enjoyed riding and there was plenty of scope for this at Ravenscroft, indeed the Kent School Stables are still nearby on Skiff Mountain.

Melvin must have had this proposal in mind for some time. He probably asked if he could return to UK via USA and, given his family connections and his suitability for attachment to the RAF Delegation in Washington, this would have been reasonable. He warned Priscilla that his duties in the RAF had been very hazardous and would probably be so again. Nonetheless, he wanted very much to get married and she was the lady of his choice.

The day of Monday, 10 August, was chosen for the wedding, to be held in the Chapel at Kent School with a reception at Ravenscroft Farm afterwards. The new headmaster of Kent, Father Chalmers OHC, agreed to officiate. Melvin had seen Father Sill but he would not be available and was in poor health. Both Melvin and Priscilla knew Father Chalmers and liked him very much.

The female side of the Rawson family now entered a period of great excitement and activity, making preparations. In a letter to his mother, Melvin remarked that Priscilla's mother, Clementine, who much preferred her nickname 'Kempchen' and was sometimes also referred to by herself and others as 'Mother Rawson', was beside herself with excitement. From correspondence between Clementine and Father Sill it is clear that 'Mother Rawson' had maintained a deep affection for Melvin, expressing great concern at the news of his ditching experiences. During this period of pre-wedding preparation, which included a two day trip to New York City to buy a wedding dress, ring and other necessities, 'Kempchen' teased Priscilla by asking 'Is this girl who is marrying Melvin worthy of him?' Priscilla admitted that she had always fancied marrying an Englishman...'And haven't I got a handsome one?'

Melvin had told his mother that he planned to book a flight out to California to see her. He had not mentioned his plan to propose to Priscilla, indeed he admitted that he was intent on doing this before he saw his mother, whom he expected would press the merits of several Californian girls on him. It seems that he sent the surprise news of his forthcoming marriage via his Aunt Floss, Fannie's sister Florence, also known as Susie, asking her to 'break the news gently'. From a letter sent to his mother just before the wedding, he was clearly apprehensive that Fannie would be upset and was greatly relieved to receive a cable to say that she too was very happy. His adopted brother Dodd, then fourteen and with Fannie in California, recalled that 'she took it rather well'. In the same letter to Fannie, dated 7 August, Melvin admitted 'I am feeling somewhat exhausted mentally and bodily after the most eventful 5 days of my life, which had been preceded by 6 days flying from Egypt.' The news was sweetened for Fannie because Melvin and Priscilla were to fly to Los Angeles immediately after the wedding, on a TWA schedule which would have them arrive at Burbank airport on Tuesday morning. In his letter to Fannie, Melvin had said 'I am so happy I cannot begin to tell you, but I know you will love my Priscilla, who is the sweetest girl I know.'

There was a great deal of telegram activity, informing friends and relations and receiving congratulations in return. Among the first to send good wishes were Aunt Bert and her sister Ethel, now both in Tunbridge Wells, although it took Melvin's father a few more days to follow suit, albeit he was very pleased. From California came good wishes from Aunt Floss and Melvin's cousin, Bob Rowan and his wife Louise. And, of course, congratulations came from a great many friends and relations of Priscilla. Melvin's sister Mary sent a cable via the Rowan Building in Los Angeles, to intercept the honeymoon in California, and included news that Angela had passed her exams. All these telegrams were carefully saved and placed in an album by Clementine, along with carefully typed lists of wedding presents and letters of thanks. The wedding present list was extensive, consisting of typical household items, money and silverware.

This wartime wedding was a relatively small affair – most young men were away in the services and the location at Ravenscroft, Priscilla's much loved home, is somewhat remote. Ed Rawson, as a long time friend, acted as best man, becoming brother-in-law as the ceremony progressed. Ed's poor eyesight precluded him from service in the armed forces and, in his modest way, he said 'I was available' but he would, no doubt, have been an easy choice for Melvin anyway. Priscilla wore a long, flowing white dress and veil. She was supported by two close friends, Margie Newton and Barbara Magaletta, also in elegant light coloured dresses, as bridesmaids.

The wedding ceremony took place in the fine stone built St Joseph's Chapel at Kent School; Father W.S. Chalmers OHC officiated and provided a handwritten marriage certificate reading:

> In the Name of the Father and of the Son
> and of the Holy Ghost. Amen.
> this is to certify that I
> joined in Holy Matrimony
> Melvin Young
> and
> Priscilla Rawson
> in St Joseph's Chapel of Kent School
> on August tenth, nineteen hundred and
> forty two.
> May God bless and protect you both,
> and, having his holy way with you, bring
> you to that life and joy which is eternal
> > W S Chalmers OHC
> > The Feast of Saint Lawrence,
> > Kent, Connecticut, USA

The wedding party then drove the few miles up to Skiff Mountain for the reception at Ravenscroft Farm. The formal photographs were taken at the rear of that fine, old New England farmhouse. Less formal pictures show Melvin leading Priscilla out of the house, Melvin taking one of Priscilla, still in her wedding dress, with Ed and Priscilla's Aunt Dorothy in the garden. The honeymoon was about to start with a long, eighteen hour, five stop flight to California, and there is a 'going away' snap, showing Melvin in uniform and Priscilla in day clothes, about to get in a car. The boot is open for the luggage and Priscilla's wire haired terrier, Mickey, looked rather sad, probably aware from all the excitement that 'something was up'.

The newly weds were then driven to New York to catch the 8.30 p.m. (Eastern Time) TWA 'Sky Chief' Flight 7 to Los Angeles. A note on the timetable tells us that the fare was $149.95 plus $7.50 tax. This service, apparently using Douglas DC-3 aircraft, made stops at Pittsburgh (10.44 p.m., ET), Chicago (12.47 a.m., Central Time), Kansas City (3.51 a.m., CT), Amarillo (7.12 a.m., CT), Albuquerque (8.12 a.m., Mountain Time) and was due to arrive at Los Angeles, Burbank Airport at 11.33 a.m., Pacific Time. This was Priscilla's first ever flight in any aircraft and was a very tiring introduction to the air. Melvin, by contrast, had plenty of opportunity to compare notes with the TWA pilots.

On arrival at Burbank, Melvin and Priscilla were met by Fannie and Aunt Floss, who had offered the newly weds the use of the ranch, Cielito Lindo, which Melvin knew well, and the family cabin on Big Bear Lake. However first, there was lunch in Los Angeles before retiring, very tired to the ranch. Announcements and reports of the wedding featured in newspapers on both sides of the American continent, in the *New York Times* and *Herald Tribune*, the *Los Angeles Examiner* and in the society column of another Californian paper. The latter announced that the couple had been 'honeymooning quietly in Southern California' and 'spent the first week of their stay here at the country home of the bridegroom's aunt, Miss Florence Rowan'.

The Times, in London, carried an announcement somewhat later, on 17 September. It read:

YOUNG:RAWSON – On August 10, 1942, in Kent School Chapel, Kent, Conn., USA, by the Rev. W. S. Chalmers OHC. SQUADRON LEADER HENRY MELVIN YOUNG, DFC, RAFVR to PRISCILLA, only daughter of Mr & Mrs

HOBART RAWSON of Ravenscroft Farm, Kent, Conn., and 22 East 36th Street, New York.

We must feel some sympathy for Priscilla, being introduced to her new relations after an exciting few days and a very long and noisy flight across the continent. She tended to suffer from travel sickness and found the 100 mile journey to Big Bear Lake, high up in the San Bernardino Mountains, where the peaks range up to about 10,000 feet, very tiring. The last part of the journey was along twisting mountain roads. The 'cabin', actually quite a substantial house, was in a picturesque setting perhaps 100 feet above the lake.

This was certainly a very romantic place for a honeymoon, although the newly-weds were not entirely alone. The photographs show that Aunt Floss and Fannie were there some of the time and Dodd Young had a vacation job looking after boats on the dock. He recalled spending some time with Melvin. One picture shows Melvin and Priscilla relaxing in the cabin, with a typewriter prominent on a table. Melvin's handwriting was rather cramped and sometimes difficult to decipher – the left hander writing with his right hand – and he had promised Fannie that he would get back to using a typewriter as soon as possible.

All good things must come to an end, and soon enough it was time to return to the east coast. The send-off for Melvin and Priscilla was from Aunt Floss' house in Los Angeles. Floss was so delighted with the marriage that 'she could not have been more pleased if it were her own'. She never married, being the 'rock' who looked after the rest of the family. On the way back, however, Melvin and Priscilla broke their journey at Albuquerque, New Mexico, and enjoyed a brief visit to the mountains in that state. In a letter to Fannie on Sunday 30 August from Ravenscroft, he recounted that:

Pris[1] was feeling pretty seedy all the return journey and was sick once or twice, but we were met by her Aunt[2] who held her hand and we fed her tea with drops of brandy at the Grand Central[3] and she was much better by the time we got to the train, and that was air conditioned, so she felt quite well when we arrived at Kent, and ate a large dinner and got a good nights sleep and is herself again.

And so, on 31 August, Melvin and Priscilla set off for Washington DC. He was not sure what duties would be assigned and thought he might be sent to Canada. They stayed in Washington at the Cosmos Club. Priscilla's uncle, Clementine's brother, worked in Washington for the Bureau of Standards and was a member of this club, which catered for scientists and technical professionals, and he made the necessary introductions. Melvin described it to his mother, in a letter on 6 September, as 'just on one side of the square in front of the White House and a very pleasant spot indeed, and somewhat of a highbrow club'. He continued this letter saying 'The Air Vice Marshal came to dinner with us and charmed and was charmed by Priscilla and last night we had dinner with him at the University Club and met the Air Marshal, the head of the RAF Delegation, and had a very pleasant evening.' At that time the Head of the RAF Delegation was Sir Douglas Evill, and his deputy was Air Vice Marshal William MacNeece Foster.

Air Vice Marshal Foster was educated at Cheltenham College and the Royal Military Academy at Sandhurst, and won the DSO in 1917, the DFC in 1918 and was made an honorary MA by Oxford University in 1941. He had published *An Airman's Te Deum*, printed in 1936 to music by Sir Walford Davies and, in 1937, to music by Dr Martin Shaw. In later life, 1966-7, he became Lord Mayor of Oxford. Clearly he would have had plenty in common with Melvin and Priscilla to make good dinner conversation.

It now seemed that the plan for Melvin was to spend two or three weeks in the southern States of the USA giving talks to the US Army Air Corps – a prospect which he described as 'rather alarming but might be quite fun'. Meanwhile, while waiting for Air Ministry permission for these lectures, he and Priscilla were able to relax and enjoy the late summer in Washington. He told Fannie that he regretted not having found a present to send for her birthday, a few days later, 'but expect I shall be coerced into having my photograph taken and when I do that will be your belated birthday present'. There is indeed a portrait photograph from this period, but Fannie and Angela always preferred a less formal picture, taken by William L. White on HMS *St Mary's*, in which, not surprisingly, Melvin had a very cheerful smile!

He ended this letter to Fannie on 6 September, by telling her that he had had a 'Very nice letter from Father and Punkie,[4] P. very breezy and nice to Priscilla too.' In a postscript he asked his mother 'If you haven't done so, it would make me very happy if you would write to Father, having seen Priscilla, as he has not, and tell him what you will of her, if you don't object too much.' Clearly he was on good terms with both his parents and did not know that they had divorced. The stigma of divorce was such, especially in some circles, that they kept this from all their children; indeed Melvin died unaware that his parents had actually divorced. It seems that Henry and Fannie maintained a relationship after the tensions of the divorce, and even tried a reconciliation in the late 1940s, but unsuccessfully.

The RAF Delegation (RAFDEL) was part of the British Air Commission to the USA and was located at 1424 16th Street NW in Washington DC. The UK National Archives at Kew have little information relevant to Melvin at this time, apart from a signal from the Air Ministry to RAFDEL on 10 September which said:

> No objection to retention of S/L H M Young for one month commencing day following termination of leave.[5] Request date of effect when we will promulgate attachment of YOUNG to your delegation for temporary duty.

Another telegram on 18 September said, rather belatedly:

> Attachment of S/L H M Young to RAFDEL with effect from 31 July authorised. Retention until 29 September agreed.[6]

Melvin then spent two weeks in Florida addressing members of the US Army Air Corps An article in the *Tampa Daily Times* on Tuesday 22 September was headed 'Veteran RAF Flyer on Army Program at MacDill Field'. It went on to announce that Squadron Leader H.M. Young, veteran RAF flier, will appear at MacDill Field Thursday as part of the Army orientation program.' The lecture was to be entitled 'Night Bombing

Operations – Germany, Sicily, Libya' and his story would be one
of personal participation. A brief personal history of Melvin and
his operational career was also included.

A subsequent report was headed 'RAF OFFICER TELLS
MACDILL MEN OF RAIDS' with a sub-heading 'Says Anti-
Aircraft Fire Improves in Germany'. This report reads:

> Flying crews at MacDill Field got some pointers on bombing
> technique yesterday from an RAF officer who has taken part
> in more than 50 raids on enemy territory in Europe and
> Africa.
>
> Squadron Leader H M Young, winner of the distinguished
> flying cross, in two talks at the MacDill theatre, told how
> RAF planes go about the regular night-time job of bombing
> German cities and how the Germans are making it tough for
> them.
>
> Anti-aircraft fire is much harder to get through now than
> it was a year ago, the officer said. Germans also have
> adopted the trick of building fires in fields after the first
> wave of bombers goes over, to lead succeeding bombers
> astray from their target.

Italian Gunners Hid

> The RAF pilot said that after the British made their first raid
> on Italy they learned from intelligence reports that many of
> the Italian anti-aircraft gunners had hid in air raid shelters
> during the attack instead of manning their guns.
>
> 'We heard there was a mass execution of the gunners as a
> result of the raid' he added.
>
> In striking targets in Italy, the British squadrons had to fly
> over Switzerland. 'We could look down and see the homes
> lighted up in Swiss towns.' Young said 'It gave us a happy
> feeling, coming from a land that had been blacked out for a
> year and a half.'

After this interlude in Florida, Melvin was able to get a weekend
at Kent at the end of September, no doubt to Priscilla's pleasure.
He was invited to attend a Sunday night supper at Kent School
and address the boys in the Dining Hall, which remains largely

unchanged to this day, although extended. Melvin, in his RAF uniform, gave the following address. As reported in the *Kent School News*, he was 'calm and deliberate', after which he met members of the Sixth Form in the Study and answered their questions:

I have spent two weeks talking to the United States Air Force [*sic*], stationed in Florida' Squadron Leader Young began, and referring jokingly to the noise in the Dining Hall, went on to say: 'I am afraid talking to you here will be worse for me. Down there my audience was subject to military discipline.'

I have always had a great fright in speaking at all. Once in England my C.O. told me that I would have to deliver a talk on bombing to some pongos[7] of the 'bloody infantry'. Thinking they would all be young I made very little preparation on my speech, and it was with uneasiness that I discovered I was about to speak to high ranking infantry officers.

Started Flying at Oxford

I started flying at Oxford University. They had a flying squadron there, and I was in the reserves until war broke out and I was called. I believe it was exactly three years ago today. I had always been a clumsy oarsman, both at Kent and Oxford, and my instructors found me clumsy flying. So I was detailed to fly a bomber. Flying a bomber is not unlike being the middle man in an eight-oared shell.

I have made many flights over enemy territory since the war began. One night over Kiel we were caught in the searchlights, and on the way home we had to fly low. Passing over Denmark we were flying so low that a man in a farm house pulled his blind down when he saw us coming.

My reputation for always wanting to row is bad in the Air Force. Several times I have had to park my plane in the sea and take to the rubber boats. My friends cautioned me that it was a rather expensive way of brushing up on my rowing.

On one occasion we sent an SOS before we crash-landed in

the sea, and thought they would hear us and pick us up. The woman in the auxiliary at home who caught our message somehow put it in the files, and while we all sat in our rubber boat, our distress signal lay resting in a file for future reference. Fortunately we had a bottle of rum with us. After twenty-four hours an American destroyer which you sent over sighted us. We finished the rum and felt a good deal better.

Bombs Italy

I was in the first bombing trip from England to Italy. The trip across the Alps was most beautiful. Flying across Germany we had been used to fighting it out, but in Italy we met no opposition. It seems that when the Italian anti-aircraft gunners heard us coming, they ran for the air-raid shelters. So while the Italian Command was busy court-martialling their soldiers, we managed to drop our load and slip away.

My last months were spent in the Mediterranean, both in Malta and in Egypt. We didn't think much of being a bomber squadron in Malta, the place was most bombed. Our target was Naples, and flying trips over that target afforded our navigators an easy time, for on a clear day Naples can be seen from fifty miles away.

We were sent next to Egypt. It was rotten there, with the sand and flies. They finally decided it was time for me to come home. I was very fortunate in being able to return to England through the United States. I shall be flying a bomber back in England soon.

It has been ten years since I have been here, and it is needless to say that I am happy to be back. I hope that everyone didn't have trouble hearing me at the other end of the Dining Hall. My only speaking experience has been shouting at crews on the river from the towpaths. It's an excellent way to learn to speak.

Afterwards, Melvin wrote to Father Chalmers:

I hadn't time to think up what to say to the school about anything other than bombs, and I didn't want to talk much about them. I had just been to Sunday evening chapel after so many years and it made me very happy and very profoundly grateful to be there again in the old familiar scene and hear the hymns I know of old. It was very far from war and I couldn't talk much about bombs right after.

I was very glad to be able to see school again, and in such spirits. I had forgotten that there was such a difference from an English school. The American boy has a lot less reserve and is free from too strong a sense of decorum that inflicts the English school. I was startled at first and it took a little time to feel at home but I wouldn't have missed it for anything.

From Melvin's references to his own reticence in speaking we might suspect that, had he survived the war to resume his legal studies, he would have been more inclined to be a solicitor, like his father, than a barrister acting as advocate for a client to a jury. However, he would have more speeches to make. His next posting, on 15 October, was to the Twin-Engined Advanced Flying Training School at Turner Field, Albany, Georgia, where many RAF pilots honed their skills under what was known as the 'Arnold scheme', named after the US General of that name. Albany is in the south-western part of Georgia, some seventy miles north of Florida and fifty miles east of Alabama. The record shows[8] that the Turner Field Advanced School achieved graduation rates around 90 per cent for the period when Melvin was there. Significantly no trainees were recorded as being killed; probably a reflection of operating in better weather conditions than would have been the case in Britain.

Melvin's duties here seem to have been varied but included speaking at an event entitled 'Alabama's Contribution to Victory'. This seems to have been held in Birmingham, Alabama, and Melvin was programmed to make an address entitled 'I Saw It Happen'. He is also recorded in a local newspaper photograph, congratulating a British trainee and presenting a certificate; the caption reads:

This young British flier receiving his wings from Squadron Leader H.M. Young, British Liaison officer, may be thinking of the last time he saw England. Then his country was barely holding its own with the Nazis. Now with the American troops they are battering the panzers in Africa. Though they fight under a burning African sun or sullen Russian skies, these Turner graduates will be certain to carry on the heroic traditions of the RAF. This young man saw the horrors of the blitz; now he is ready to pay it back in kind.

The reference to American troops in Africa suggest that the date of this presentation was after the Operation Torch landings in North Africa which started on 8 November 1942.

Priscilla was able to accompany Melvin on this posting to Georgia and took part in the social life at the airbase, joining the Turner Field Women's Club which met at the Officers' Club; wives of all officers at Turner Field were automatically members. On 4 December, the RAF officers threw a cocktail party (6 to 8 p.m.) in the Turner Field Officers' Club for their US colleagues and the many friends they had made in the locality. The invitation to Captain Arvid Taube, Commandant of Cadets, and his wife, survives. It was undoubtedly a bonus for Melvin to have Priscilla with him for such an occasion.

Priscilla's dog seems to have accompanied them to Georgia; the dog is recorded, under his pedigree name, Mickey Ley Byford, as coming first in the Novice category for Wire Terriers, and in one photograph Melvin is seen about to enter a car with a taut dog lead in his hand. Mickey was out of shot.

While the couple were in Georgia, Fannie travelled by train from California to see them. This was a long journey and Fannie carried gifts, including prize California oranges, to save the newly-weds having to eat inferior ones from Florida!

The couple were able to send their family and friends RAF Christmas cards that year. Significantly the message printed was 'With Every Good Wish for a Happy Christmas and **Brighter** New Year' and was from the 'Royal Air Force Serving with Southeast Army Air Forces Training Center, United States of America'.

Melvin wrote to Father Chalmers at Kent in January[9] telling him that he and Priscilla had a 'very quiet Christmas, church at midnight Christmas eve, listening to the Empire Broadcast and the King's Speech in the morning, attending the Cadets dinner at midday for me and our own dinner in the evening'. He explained the tradition in the British services that officers serve the men dinner on Christmas day:

> An enormous meal was provided and the RAF Administrative Officer and the RAF Officer instructors and myself helped wait at table and served beer to the cadets. It seemed a far cry to my last Christmas spent in Malta and I certainly never expected then to spend this one in Georgia.

Melvin went on to say that he had been to Clewiston (Florida) to visit his friend Wing Commander Prickett who had travelled with him from Africa. Thomas Prickett was now Commanding Officer of a British Flying Training School at Clewiston, which is in southern Florida on Lake Okeechobee 400 miles from Albany – he recalled that Melvin had visited one day – it would have made a good cross country training flight! Prickett told Melvin that he had a Kent boy, Dudley Amoss (Class of 40 and an oarsman at Henley in 1939), who had lost the tip of a finger and had been judged ineligible for flying by the US Army Air Corps, but had been accepted for pilot training by the RAF and was doing well. Amoss went on to a distinguished career as a combat pilot.

Tom Prickett remembered 'Dinghy' Young as:

> ...a great character, an Anglo-American, an Oxford Rowing Blue. A very determined character with lots of charm. I was proud to know him and was very sad when he was killed in the Dams Raid.

He also recalled that when they arrived in the USA, Melvin had telephoned his mother in California who was a friend of the parents of Tom's future wife, Elizabeth, who lived in Laguna Beach. Tom Prickett waited until his movements were clear before he, too, telephoned California, and received a 'severe rebuke' for not calling sooner – but they got married in September anyway and enjoyed a long and happy marriage.[10]

Melvin also mentioned Captain (later Major) Arvid Taube (Kent, Class of 13) who was the Commandant of Cadets at

Turner Field 'having formerly done an excellent job of work in charge of the coloured troops'. This was still a time when colour segregation was normal in the southern states. Arvid E Taube had been one of the first graduates of Kent School and went on to be a member of the Class of 1917 at Princeton University, but he did not graduate as he went to serve in the US Army Balloon Corps in the First World War.[11] Melvin explained to Father Chalmers that he had been kept very busy at Turner Field, with the title of RAF Liaison Officer, giving some lectures and doing quite a lot of flying instruction 'with our RAF boys'. He commented that he had been very happy there and found all the American officers exceptionally friendly and helpful. However, 'the last of the British cadets training under the Arnold scheme leave next month and my job will be ending in a few weeks time'. Indeed within two weeks he was on his way to England, to bomber operations as he wished. Melvin ended his letter by asking Father Chalmers to be the first American recipient should any bad news be sent by his father and to break it to the Rawson family, and Priscilla in particular, as he (Father Chalmers) saw fit.

From a surviving family album it seems that Melvin and Priscilla also spent some time at Maxwell Field, Alabama. However, from December 1942 until the end of January 1943, they were in Albany, having taken an apartment there. A photograph shows Melvin carrying two suitcases down a flight of stairs from the apartment to load in a car belonging to the Rawson family on their departure. Priscilla had the use of this car in Georgia and, since her brother Edward was unlikely to need it in Washington, the plan was to take it back to Ravenscoft, where her parents were to retire from their New York apartment later that year. After Melvin's departure for Britain Priscilla spent some of her time at The College Club, 40 Commonwealth Avenue, Boston. Until their retirement her parents were not always at Ravenscroft, and she lived in Boston on and off for much of her life, enjoying the musical and intellectual attractions of that city.

Melvin said his final goodbye to Priscilla in New York on 2 February 1943 – the end of their married life together – and set off by train to Boston on the first stage of his journey to England. This was also a momentous day on the Eastern Front. The Battle of Stalingrad ended with the surrender of 40,000 German troops and the tide of war started to flow firmly against Germany, but there was much danger yet to come. This American interlude must rank as one of the happiest times of Melvin's life – it undoubtedly fortified him for a return to the hardships of war in England and the hazards of operational flying.

Notes
1. All the family called her this.
2. Dorothy, staying with Clementine at Ravenscroft from her home in Nantucket.
3. Grand Central Rail Terminus.
4. His sister Mary.
5. 30 August.
6. No corresponding signals going from RAFDEL to the Air Ministry were found at Kew.
7. Air Force slang for Army officers.
8. National Archives AIR 15/11.
9. Letter from H.M. Young to Father Chalmers, 17 January 1943.
10. Private correspondence from Air Chief Marshal Sir Thomas Prickett KCB DSO DFC RAF Retired.
11. Private correspondence with Major Taube's daughter, Margaret Taube Harper.

Chapter 9

Operation Chastise – The Dams Raid

When Melvin left the USA at the beginning of February 1943 he did not know what fate and the RAF had in store for him, except that he expected, and wanted, to return to operational flying. His life story would have been interesting enough anyway, given his transatlantic background and schooling, his rowing successes and his already distinguished flying career. The climax of his life which now unfolded saw him take a central role in arguably the most famous single action of the RAF, Operation Chastise. Sadly it was to cost his life and those of fifty two other young flyers.

Operation Chastise, the 'Dambuster Raid' has been the subject of numerous books, articles, TV features and one famous cinema film. This biography does not attempt to repeat previous work, rather to record how it was for Melvin Young and his immediate colleagues. The author has attempted to analyse the technical and operational aspects to the best of his ability. As for the value of the raid the author can only repeat some words he wrote for the Trinity College, Oxford, Report (2003):

Operation Chastise, the Raid on the Ruhr Dams on the night of 16/17 May 1943, was an epic of courage, determination and ingenuity. The physical effect on Germany's war effort was serious, although less than strategic planners had hoped. However, the moral, political and psychological impact was great, at a time when victory was unsure and distant. Churchill, in Washington at the time, was able to point to this remarkable feat of arms as a signal success.

How Melvin travelled from the USA to England is not recorded, although his record of service shows him transferred to the 'general register' of RAF Uxbridge from 3 February 1943. He had at this time been away from operations over northern Europe for some two years, excepting a very limited period with 104 Squadron at Driffield in October 1941, and had yet to be introduced to the heavy four-engined bombers such as the Avro Lancaster. This introduction came in the first half of March at 1654 Conversion Unit (CU), Wigsley, and 1660 CU, Swinderby; both these airfields lie between Newark-on-Trent and Lincoln. Melvin is recorded in the 1654 ORB[1] as arriving at Wigsley on 1 March and then makes no further mention of him. According to his record of service he was posted the next day to Swinderby. These conversion units operated the Lancaster and its less successful, twin-engined predecessor the Avro Manchester. Unfortunately the ORB for 1660 CU[2] has no entries for March 1943, but Melvin's conversion to heavy bombers must have gone well enough, because the log book of Flying Officer Rupert Oakley, an instructor at 1654 CU Wigsley, records a twenty minute flight commander's test flight with Melvin and six crew in Manchester L7453 on 12 March 1943[3]

The Avro Lancaster was a large aircraft by the standards of its day. The wingspan was 102 feet and the maximum weight was 63,000lbs (28 tons). Take-off at this weight needed a long run and was a fraught experience – lift off speed was 105 mph, but the take-off safety speed was 130 mph, below which engine failure would make control very difficult, so there was a period of hazard while the aircraft accelerated, the crew praying that all four Rolls-Royce Merlin engines kept going. It might be said that the Lancaster was about twice the aircraft that the Wellington – Melvin's previous 'mount' – was. There was no power assistance to the controls but they were described in the *Pilot's Notes* as being 'relatively light and effective', becoming heavy in turns (elevators) or at high speeds. It was sufficiently complicated to require a flight engineer to manage the four engines and other systems. Generally it was regarded as a good, 'pilot's aircraft'; one ATA lady pilot[4] once described it to the author as being like a 'large Anson' and coming from the Avro stable this seems reasonable. It was not designed with low level operations such as Operation Chastise in mind and it is a tribute to its designers, led by Roy Chadwick, that it performed as well as it did under a range of circumstances.

It was common practice for crews to come together, by a process of mutual agreement, at Conversion Units. It seems likely that Melvin met his crew at 1660 CU at Swinderby. The 1660 CU Operational Record Book (ORB) shows that five of them (Horsfall, Beesley, Nichols, Yeo and Ibbotson) had flown together on an operation to Berlin on 16/17 January, with Pilot Officer V. Duxbury DFC as pilot and Flight Lieutenant T.W. Blair as navigator. Some nineteen aircraft from various CUs were detailed to attack Berlin, but for technical reasons only three, including the above crew, succeeded – bombs were aimed at red markers laid by Pathfinder aircraft and were seen to burst across these 'red cascades'. The flak over the target was heavy but inaccurate. The following night David Horsfall flew with Flying Officer H.W. Southgate on another raid to Berlin, when they bombed an estimated position over solid cloud cover. Horsfall would have gained some useful experience since the return flight from the Dutch coast was made on three engines 'as the starboard inner cut'.

Melvin's original crew were all sergeants:

David Horsfall – flight engineer

Charles Roberts – navigator

Lawrence Nichols – wireless operator

Gordon Yeo – air gunner

Wilfred Ibbotson – air gunner

The original bomb aimer was probably John Beesley, but for some reason he was judged unsuitable for 617 Squadron and a Canadian, Flying Officer Vincent MacCausland, was drafted into the crew. Beesley was later shot down on a raid with another squadron and became a prisoner of war.

On 13 March Melvin and his new crew were posted to 57

Melvin leads his bride out of Ravenscroft.

Melvin photographs Priscilla, Edward and their Aunt Dorothy at the wedding reception.

Priscilla and Melvin prepare to leave Ravenscroft on honeymoon after their wedding, 10 August 1942. Mickey, Priscilla's terrier, knows 'something is up'.

Aunt Florence's ranch 'Cielito Lindo', near Los Angeles.

Melvin and Aunt Floss, at the ranch, August 1942.

Priscilla, Melvin and a typewritter on honeymoon at the cabin on Big Bear Lake, California.

Melvin, Aunt Floss and Priscilla at the Big Bear 'cabin'.

The Cabin (upper building in picture) from Big Bear Lake.

Priscilla and Melvin in Aunt Floss' garden in Los Angeles just before departing for the East Coast at the end of the honeymoon.

Squadron Leader Henry Melvin Young RAFVR, DFC and Bar. Portrait photograph in USA, September 1942. Sent to his mother for her birthday.

Melvin Young boarding a TWA aircraft, USA 1942.

Dining hall at Kent School where Melvin addressed the students in September 1942. Father Sill's portrait looks on. (Author 2006)

Melvin Young addressing an audience in the USA, 1942.

Melvin carries luggage from the apartment in Albany, Georgia, before leaving for the UK.

Officers Mess, RAF Scampton. (Author 2006)

Eyebrook Reservoir, near Uppingham. Much used for Operation *Chastise* training. (Author 2003)

Abberton Reservior near Colchester. Also used for *Chastise* training, including the 'Dress Rehearsal'. (Author 2003)

A 'Dambuster' Lancaster releases an UPKEEP weapon during trials off the Kent coast, May 1943. (IWM FLM 2365)

The Mohne Dam, early on 17 May 1943. Water is still flowing through the breach. Taken by a Photographic Reconnaissance Spitfire. (IWM CH9687)

Mohne Dam from North end - darker concrete shows repaired section. (Author 2004)

Edersee from the Dam - Waldeck Castle top right - the difficult terrain is apparent. (Author 2004)

Eder Dam as repaired - lighter coloured concrete shows where off-centre breach occurred. (Author 2004)

German photograph of Lancaster wreckage on the Dutch beach. Thought to be AJ-A. (The National Archives, ref. AIR20/4367)

The Melvin Young Room, Kent School, Connecticut, with Melvin's school photograph and a memorial plaque above the fireplace. (Author 2005)

Melvin's entry in the Westminster School Book of Remembrance. (Author 2006, by permission of the Governing Body of Westminster School)

617 Squadron Memorial, Woodhall Spa, Lincolnshire. (Author 2006)

The Graves of Melvin Young and four of his crew members, Bergen General Cemetery, North Holland. (Author 2006)

Melvin Young's Headstone at Bergen, North Holland. (Author 2006)

Family gathering in England 1948. Middle row: Clementine Rawson (far left), Priscilla (third from left) next to Mary Young. Front row: Angela (second from left), Bridget Nendick, god-daughter (far right). (Mrs Bridget Corby)

Squadron at Scampton, a pre-war RAF aerodrome with the usual complement of permanent buildings, four miles north of Lincoln. Coincidentally, the Station Commander at Scampton was Group Captain J.N.H. 'Charles' Whitworth, who had been Melvin's flying instructor in the Oxford University Air Squadron. Before Melvin could take part in any operations with 57 Squadron he was caught up in the urgent formation of a new squadron which was to undertake a special operation and then be available for other unusual bombing tasks. For some years pre-war the RAF's strategic planners had determined that the destruction of the large dams supplying water to the Ruhr Valley steel industry might have a very great effect on German war production – many tons of water are required to produce a ton of steel. Also the consequent flooding would do a lot of damage and some hydro-electric power would be lost. There were several dams supplying the Ruhr, of which the Möhne Dam was the most important. This dam was, and indeed still is, having been rebuilt, an imposing, massive structure. To hit it with a sufficiently large, well aimed conventional bomb dropped from high altitude was beyond the technology then available. Various ingenious alternative ways of attacking the dams were put forward but none showed much promise until Dr Barnes Wallis, of Vickers-Armstrong Ltd and designer of the Wellington bomber, devised a system for skipping a large depth charge along the surface of the water, thus clearing the anti-torpedo nets defending the water face of the dam, to hit the dam, roll down in contact with the wall and detonate 3 tons of high explosive 30 feet down. The water would concentrate the shock wave on the masonry and cause it to collapse.

This system was, of course, specifically designed to attack masonry dams of which there were several in the Ruhr area. However, the second most important dam serving the Ruhr was the Sorpe; this was of a later type with shallow sloping earth faces on each side of a concrete core, for which the weapon was not ideal, albeit it was to be used with a different technique. In the event the planners decided to make the second priority target the Eder Dam, some forty-six miles south-east of the Möhne. This was also a large masonry, gravity dam and held back the water of the largest reservoir in Germany. It did not supply the Ruhr industry but its destruction would do much flood damage and reinforce the message that Bomber Command could make devastating precision strikes. Other, less important, targets on the list for attack were the Lister, Diemel and Ennepe Dams.

A series of experiments and flight trials produced a plan which required this weapon, code named Upkeep, to be released under quite specific circumstances; about 450 yards from the dam, at 220 mph and at 60 feet above the water. The weapon, which was a cylinder carried under specially modified Lancasters, was to be spun backwards to aid the skipping process and help to keep it in contact with the water face of the dam as it sank to its detonation depth. All this is easily written but not easily achieved and the idea received much scepticism, not least from Air Marshal Sir Arthur 'Bomber' Harris, Commander-in-Chief of Bomber Command. However Sir Charles Portal, the Chief of the Air Staff was in favour of trying to break the dams, not least because it would be a great boost to morale and to Britain's standing with her allies, being able to mount a precision blow on a notable target. Thus a special Squadron was to be set up within 5 Group, Bomber Command, under the command of Air Vice Marshal The Hon. Sir Ralph Cochrane, to make this attack. The timescale was short, less than two months, since the lakes would be full in mid May when a full moon would enable the crews to have a chance of success. The operation would be flown at the lowest possible height to reduce the risk of being identified by radar and intercepted by night fighters.

The new squadron was soon allocated the now famous number 617; still a leading strike squadron in the RAF. The man designated by Harris to command the squadron and lead the attack was Wing Commander Guy Penrose Gibson. Gibson was born in India in 1918, the son of a British official, and grew up in the 'Raj' – the family were used to having numerous, deferential servants and in due course Guy was sent home to England to boarding school, principally at St Edward's School in Oxford. From there he joined the RAF and became a distinguished bomber and night fighter pilot, with a DSO and Bar and a DFC and Bar. He was short in stature, but energetic, determined and aggressive – Harris regarded him as the archetypal warrior. These qualities would be needed to mount Operation Chastise in the time available.

Personnel

The plan for recruiting aircrew personnel for 617 Squadron was that, as far as possible, they should be from within 5 Group and should be from crews who had completed two operational tours.[5] In practice they were a 'mixed bunch'; some were known to Gibson and transferred at his request, for example from 106 Squadron, his previous squadron. Others were moved as was convenient to the Group. In Melvin's case, his 'C' Flight of 57 Squadron was posted *in toto* across the station on 25 March. Possibly Charles Whitworth had recommended that Melvin should be considered for the new 'special squadron' that was forming on his base.

These 'C' Flight crews were led by Melvin, Flight Lieutenant William (Bill) Astell, Pilot Officer Geoff Rice and Flight Sergeant Ray Lovell. They had not volunteered for this unknown assignment. Rice protested but to no avail. Lovell was posted back to 57 Squadron after two weeks – 'the crew did not come up to the standards necessary for this squadron'. Like Melvin, Astell had been a Wellington pilot in Egypt, with 148 Squadron; a twenty-three year old Mancunian, he had survived a crash-landing in the desert after being attacked by a German night fighter over Derna, started walking back and was picked up by a British Army advanced reconnaissance unit and returned to his squadron. Bill Astell was awarded the DFC in August 1942.[6] At least there was a bonus for these ex-57 Squadron officers that they did not have to move from Scampton's substantial mess accommodation.

Given Melvin's experience of administration and training, in the Middle East and the USA, it was natural that he should have been made one of the two flight commanders. He was to take much of the load from Gibson in organizing the heavy training programme which was necessary. Indeed, Gibson wrote afterwards[7] that 'Melvyn [*sic*] had been responsible for a good deal of the training which made this raid possible. He had endeared himself to the boys.' Geoff Rice remarked of Melvin 'He lived with a typewriter, a fantastic administrator' – again his experience of typing was coming in useful. Gibson also wrote that Melvin could down a pint of beer faster than anyone if he chose to do so.

Flight Lieutenant Les Munro RNZAF who, although not in Melvin's flight and thus recalling social contact in the Officers Mess, remembered Melvin's tendency to sit cross legged on the floor and hold his pint round the body of the tankard, seldom by the handle. Munro also said that he found Melvin congenial by nature and easy to get on with. 'Rank was never an issue with him'.[8] Sergeant George L. 'Johnny' Johnson, McCarthy's bomb aimer, and now Squadron Leader RAF, Retd, wrote:

> My recollection is of one who was absolutely dedicated to his work but who, at the same time, had a very pleasant sense of humour. Those who knew him better spoke very highly of his first class ability as a pilot, a point which was exemplified by his two successful ditchings.[9]

Sergeant Fred E. Sutherland RCAF, Les Knight's front gunner in Maudslay's 'B' Flight, has written that Melvin:

> ...had this booming voice with an Oxford accent [perhaps more noticeable to a Canadian]. He seemed to be very popular with his fellow officers...I was an NCO, so I knew nothing of his personal life. He must have been well regarded by W/C Gibson to be selected as a Flight Commander.[10]

The second flight commander was Squadron Leader H.E. Maudslay DFC who joined 617 on 25 March from 50 Squadron, along with Australian, Pilot Officer Les Knight, and their crews. Henry Eric Maudslay, from Broadway, Worcestershire, was only twenty-one years old and had been both a middle distance runner and Captain of Boats at Eton. He was well liked, being remembered as 'a wonderful guy, a real gentleman'[11] and 'quiet, kind, purposeful – nothing was too much trouble'.[12]

Melvin and Henry Maudslay arranged the newly arrived crews into two flights. The general administration of the squadron was in the capable hands of the adjutant, Flight Lieutenant Harry R. Humphries, who had transferred to Scampton from Gibson's former 106 Squadron base at Syerston. Humphries was to be Gibson's 'right hand man' on the ground. He recalled Melvin as being rather older and quieter than the rest of the squadron, and with a habit of sitting cross legged, sometimes on his desk, which some of his flight found a bit 'off-putting'.

In Melvin's 'A' Flight were the crews led by:

Flight Lieutenant Bill Astell DFC, born in Derbyshire in 1920, joined the RAFVR in 1939 and trained in UK and Africa.

Flight Lieutenant David Maltby DFC, born at Hastings in 1920. He was training as a mining engineer pre-war. He joined the RAFVR in 1940 and trained in the UK before serving with 106 Squadron on Hampdens.

Flight Lieutenant David Shannon DFC, RAAF, born in South Australia in 1922. He joined the RAAF in 1941 and trained in Canada and then served under Guy Gibson in 106 Squadron, completing thirty-six operations.

Flight Lieutenant Robert Barlow DFC, RAAF, born in 1911 he joined the RAAF in 1941 and trained in Canada. He served with 61 Squadron on Lancasters at Syerston.

Pilot Officer Geoff Rice, born in 1917 at Portsmouth, but then lived at Hinckley, Leicestershire. He joined the RAF in 1941 and trained in the USA and Canada, arriving at 57 Squadron in December 1942.

Pilot Officer Warner Ottley DFC, born in 1923 in Battersea and grew up in Herne Bay. He joined the RAF in 1941 and trained in UK and Canada, before serving with 83 and 207 Squadrons.

Pilot Officer William Divall (replacing Flight Sergeant Lovell on 10 April 1943) joined the RAFVR in 1941 and trained in Canada and progressed via OTUs and 1660 CU at Swinderby to join 57 Squadron at Scampton in February 1943. His was one of two 617 crews who were not able to take part in Operation Chastise.

Flight Sergeant Ken Brown, RCAF, born in 1920 at Moose Jaw, Canada. He joined the RCAF in 1941 and came to the UK in 1942, joining 44 Squadron in February 1943, shortly before his transfer to 617. He eventually transferred to 6 (RCAF) Group and remained in the RCAF until 1968.

Pilot Officer Vernon Byers, RCAF, born in Star City, Saskatchewan, Canada. He joined the RCAF in 1941 and trained in Manitoba before coming to the UK and joined 467 Squadron (RAAF) in February 1943, and then 617.

Thus Melvin's flight contained a representative selection of British and Commonwealth pilots, several decorated, and with a range of experience. Other aircrew members were not always as experienced. In the squadron as a whole, the average age was twenty-three, with a range of twenty to thirty-two, and by no means all had finished two tours; some had not done one. Nonetheless there was a good cadre of experience from which Gibson could select pilots to attack the principal targets. It has been said that Bomber Command represented a microcosm of British society and 617 Squadron roughly met this description. The squadron and flight commanders were products of famous independent schools and, in Melvin's case, an American equiv-alent also, as well as Oxford. The other pilots were from a range of backgrounds but were mostly officers. The 'technical' aircrew members (flight engineers, wireless operators, gunners) generally were sergeants from various trades in civilian life. It was still an age when there was a distinct separation between officers and other ranks, and not just in the armed services. Attitudes of deference were in decline, accelerated by the war, but had some way still to fall by modern standards. The rela-tionship between aircraft captains and aircrew members varied from crew to crew. One of Melvin's sergeant crew members observed that he expected to be called 'sir' even in flight – this would be consistent with his background, but may also be a reflection of his determination to form his inexperienced crew into a disciplined unit.

It is interesting to look in more detail at the six men he welded into an efficient crew for the Dams raid.

Sergeant David Taylor Horsfall, the flight engineer, was born in Leeds in 1920. In 1936 he joined the RAF as a boy entrant at the technical apprentice school at RAF Halton and served as a ground technician until 1942 when he graduated to aircrew status. His brother, Albert, had been killed in 1940 serving as a navigator in a Hampden with 50 Squadron.

Sergeant Charles Walpole Roberts, the navigator, was born in 1921 at Cromer in Norfolk. He was a trainee accountant before joining the RAF in 1940. He was sent to Rhodesia for flying training, where, after some time at Elementary Flying Training School, he was trained as a navigator. Many would-be pilots, if they did not quickly show flying ability, were moved on to navigating. Roberts familiarity with figures would have been valuable in that role.

It is interesting to speculate whether Melvin would have been selected for further pilot training if he had joined after the start of the war, when large numbers of prospective pilots were being hurriedly screened for flying aptitude. Charles Whitworth's comment 'He is not a natural pilot' on his OUAS report is pertinent – Melvin undoubtedly became an accomplished pilot, but this was the result of his determined application to the job rather than an inherent talent.

Sergeant Lawrence William Nichols, the wireless operator, was the oldest aircrew member in the squadron having been born at Northwood, Middlesex on 17 May 1910, and thus died before dawn on his thirty-third birthday. He was married to Georgina and had joined the RAF in 1940. He trained at the RAF Signals School at Yatesbury, where Melvin had received treatment for his leg in 1939, and Air Gunners' School at Pembrey in Wales – wireless operators had to double up as gunners on some aircraft types.

Flying Officer Vincent Sandford MacCausland, the bomb aimer, was born in 1913 in Prince Edward Island and in 1940 joined the Royal Canadian Air Force, in which his brother also served. Like most Canadian aircrew he was commissioned. His role as bomb aimer also required an aptitude for navigating, especially by map reading at low level on Operation Chastise.

Sergeant Wilfred Ibbotson, the rear gunner, was born in Wakefield in 1913. He was married to Doris, who lived at Bretton West in Yorkshire, and had joined the RAF in 1941. He trained at the No. 4 Air Gunners' School at Morpeth, Northumberland and at No.10 OTU at Abingdon on Whitleys, and thus would have had this in common with Melvin.

Sergeant Gordon Alexander Yeo, the front gunner, was born at Barry, Glamorgan in 1922 and was the youngest of this older than average crew. He had joined the RAF in 1941 and was sent to No. 32 Elementary Flying Training School in Alberta, Canada. He evidently did not succeed as a pilot and eventually attended the No. 1 Air Armament School at Manby and became an air gunner.

Thus Melvin's crew averaged over twenty-seven years of age, which was old for aircrew. Three of them, including Melvin were married. Most of them had very little operational experience, and that gained at the Conversion Unit, and it must be a tribute to Melvin's determined attitude to training that, when tested on Operation Chastise, they performed well. In a letter to his parents a few days before the operation, Gordon Yeo wrote: 'You say you want to know the name of our skipper, well here it is, S/Ldr H M Young, he is not so bad lately, I expect that is because we are getting used to him, but he is the cause more or less for us not getting leave.'

On the lighter side, a month earlier Yeo had told his parents that Melvin had driven the crew into Lincoln where they watched a parade which was part of Lincoln's 'Wings for Victory' week (3-10 April) – 'we had a good laugh at the blokes all dressed up in flying clothes and sitting in the dinghy. He [Melvin] had a good laugh at them because he had detailed them.' Not for nothing was Melvin known as 'Dinghy'. Yeo also recounted how 'Larry (Nichols) our Wireless Operator went to

Windsor races last Saturday (1st May) and won about £12, but he was born lucky.' So it can be seen that although they were worked hard there was some scope for relaxation. Writing to Philip Beare after the raid, Priscilla said of Melvin '…he did speak of the especially good type of boy he had in his flight and of how much he liked his new squadron.'

Aircraft and Weapon

A specially modified version of the Lancaster was produced for Operation Chastise. It was given the rather unwieldy designation of 'Type 464 Provisioning'. The most obvious alteration from the standard aircraft was that the bomb doors had been removed and two V-shaped callipers attached to the underside of the fuselage. This structure had bearings by which the cylindrical Upkeep weapon was held, permitting rotation about its axis. The callipers were held firmly against the weapon by cables which could be released by a slip mechanism operated by the bomb aimer, when strong springs would push the callipers away, allowing the weapon to fall clear of the aircraft. On one side there was also a V-belt drive system, powered by a hydraulic motor inside the aircraft, which enabled the weapon to be spun up to the required 500 revolutions per minute (rpm) some minutes before the attack.

The Upkeep weapon was a cylinder 50 inches in diameter and just under 60 inches long (any longer would not have fitted in the aircraft). It weighed 9,250lbs (4.1 tons), of which 6,600lbs (3 tons) were high explosive. Upkeep was essentially a back-spun depth charge, and was described as such by the Germans when they examined one, although for security reasons the British called it a mine. In order to delay detonation until it had sunk to thirty feet below the water surface, it was equipped with three Admiralty type hydrostatic pistols; detonation devices which could be set to explode the charge at a preset depth. There was also a delayed action fuse which would operate ninety seconds after departure from the aircraft, to minimize the chance of an Upkeep being captured intact although, in the event, one unexploded weapon was found by the Germans.

The hydrodynamics of Upkeep have not been fully analysed

even to this day, but the principle behind the backward spin was effectively to shallow the angle of skip on contact with the water, produce a small amount of lift through the air and, very importantly, keep the weapon in contact with the water face of the dam as it sank. It was also very important that the aircraft wings were level and with no roll motion on release – no easy task – otherwise the cylinder would touch the water on one edge and veer off line. This seems to have happened with one weapon at the Möhne. On each skip, the contact with the water involved the exchange of much energy, especially the first bounce when a large plume of spray would rise dangerously close to the aircraft. Some three or four bounces could be expected, to reach the dam from the release point 425 to 475 yards away.

In order to save weight and drag, the Lancaster's mid-upper gun turret was removed. This freed the second gunner to operate the nose turret which was more likely to be useful for this raid. Another essential modification was the fitting of two spotlights, one near the nose and one at the rear of the now exposed bomb bay, which were configured to produce two circles of light on the surface below the aircraft. When these circles were touching, forming a figure of eight, the aircraft was at the prescribed height, which was reduced during experiments to a very low figure of 60 feet. The pressure altimeter in the aircraft, although a guide to the pilot, was not accurate enough for this task. The job of observing the circles of light and giving the pilot 'up, down or steady' instructions fell to the navigator during the attack; he observed the circles from the cockpit perspex blister which gave a view downwards.

The combination of removing the streamlining of the bomb doors and hanging a large cylindrical object under the aircraft, protruding into the airflow, had a marked effect on the drag of the aircraft. Trials were carried out at the Aeroplane and Armament Experimental Establishment (A&AEE) at Boscombe Down with an Upkeep 'weapon on' at a weight representative of the fuel state during the attack (60,000lbs) and 'weapon off' returning (42,500lbs). The maximum speed at 11,100 feet, 'weapon on', was 233 mph with a power setting of 3,000 rpm at

+9lb/sq.in. boost (the most available without 'going through the gate' for emergency power) – converted to 700 feet, the altitude of the Möhne Lake, this equates to a true airspeed of 199 mph in the denser air at this altitude (other factors, for example, propeller efficiency, being assumed unchanged). This probably explains why the crews had to practise diving to achieve the required 220 mph for the attack. With a cruise power setting (2650 rpm, +4 lb/sq.in. boost) the loaded aircraft achieved 206 mph at 13,600 feet, equivalent to 167 mph at sea level. The operational order for the raid specified 180 mph[13] as the transit speed to the dams but it took the section of three aircraft led by Melvin 2 hours and 26 minutes to reach the Möhne, a distance of 425 statute miles, at an average speed of 170 mph.[14] Whatever the speed achieved, the flight engineers will have been adjusting the engine controls and monitoring the fuel state very carefully.

The equivalent 'weapon off' cruise speed at the lighter weight (42,500lb) was 238 mph measured at 14,000 feet, which equates to 192 mph at sea level. Thus the return journey could be flown at higher speed, probably with less concern about fuel consumption and more concern about the approaching dawn. The log of Sergeant Nicholson, David Maltby's navigator, shows a true airspeed of 205 mph for most of the return flight. At full power (3,000 rpm and +9 lb./sq/in. boost) the returning aircraft could achieve 214 mph at sea level (256 mph measured by A&AEE at 11,600 feet), and may well have flown faster in a dive when crossing the danger area over the Dutch coast.

From the above figures it can be seen that the performance of the Type 464 Lancaster was marginal for the task allotted to it. The take-off weight was limited to 63,000lbs, so it was necessary to calculate the fuel load carefully. Apparently this job fell to Melvin though sensibly he took technical advice from the squadron engineers and the fuel carried was 1,750 gallons[15], enough for roughly seven hours flying.

Training

Initially the squadron was told to practise low level flying by day and night to achieve a high standard of navigation, mostly by clock, compass and map reading, for which the use of salient ground features was most important. Group Captain Satterly, the Senior Air Staff Officer at 5 Group, took advice on low level route finding from Group Captain E.H. 'Mouse' Fielden, MVO, AFC, who had flown many low level, special duties operations from Tempsford, Bedfordhsire, where he was now Station Commander. Fielden later became an Air Commodore and was re-appointed to his pre-war position as Captain of the King's Flight. Fielden's note of 7 April 1943[16] recommended that pinpoints were best at water features such as bends in rivers or bridges over rivers. He advised that the coast was the most dangerous place; it should be crossed as low as possible, diving to gain speed. Ironically, he suggested a pinpoint at the lake at Akersloot in Holland on the homeward route, then west to the coast – this is the place where Melvin was to be shot down!

A series of cross-country routes were devised and many of these involved flying over lakes in the Midlands and Wales. In particular, Bala Lake in Wales, the Derwent reservoir near Sheffield, the Abberton reservoir near Colchester and the Eyebrook reservoir near Corby were used. The last of these, Eyebrook, also referred to as Uppingham Lake, had been built to provide water for the nearby British steelworks! The crews did not know that they were to attack dams until the pre-flight briefing on the day of the attack – indeed Melvin and Henry Maudslay were not told until the day before – but they soon found themselves aiming at targets, on the Wainfleet bombing range (in the Wash) and at Eyebrook, which were set up to simulate the two towers on the Möhne Dam. The bomb aimers were provided with a hand-held ranging sight to tell them when to release the weapon; this used the known distance between the towers and simple trigonometry. However, some bomb aimers found this difficult to hold steady and improvised other means of measuring the dropping point. The Eyebrook reservoir was also much used to practise using the two spot-lights to get the correct height above the surface, although sometimes they were tried over the aerodrome and the waters of the Wash.

The Type 464 Lancasters were not immediately available when the squadron formed, so they were equipped with ten standard aircraft, borrowed from other squadrons, for initial training. These were pressed into service without delay. Bill Astell was sent off, on 27 March, to photograph many lakes and reservoirs all over Britain, 'on the pretext that they might be needed for training crews at Conversion Units'.[17] The next day Gibson took a Lancaster with Melvin and John Hopgood to assess their ability to fly low over water. Hopgood was one of the 'B' Flight pilots who had been with Gibson in 106 Squadron and in whom he had especial confidence, as he had helped Gibson to convert to the Lancaster. They used the Derwent reservoir and found the task very dangerous as the dusk fell. This led to the requirement for a system to measure the height accurately thus advice was taken from Farnborough where a civilian scientist, Benjamin Lockspeiser, suggested the spotlight solution.

From early in April Melvin and his crew started flying in earnest. There were many bombing runs, using small practice bombs, at the Wainfleet range and cross-country exercises around the country. On 5 April, in standard Lancaster W4921, Melvin and his crew did a 5 hour flight routing Stafford, Lake Vyrnwy, Caldey Island (Pembrokeshire), Wells (Somerset), Hunstanton (Norfolk), Wainfleet and back to Scampton. Gordon Yeo, who came from Barry in South Wales, wrote to his parents:

> We have just come back from a trip of five hours. We were flying quite close to Barry this morning. We flew right down the coast and came back round Cornwall and Bridgewater – a lovely trip. We were flying in our shirt sleeves half the time as it was so hot.

On other occasions they landed away, once at Shipdham, an American B24 base in Norfolk and once, with Geoff Rice, at Hullavington, where Melvin had done much of his training in 1940. On 19 April Melvin and his crew took the Station Commander, Charles Whitworth, and Lieutenant Marler RN, whose function and affiliation are unknown, on an exercise which included landings at Fiskerton and Marston Moor before returning to Scampton. Leonard Cheshire, Melvin's colleague from No. 9 SFTS and 102 Squadron and now a group captain, was Station Commander at Marston Moor. Cheshire flew with them on one leg of the journey. It is conjecture what Melvin and Leonard Cheshire might have discussed, but comparing notes on getting married in the USA could have been a subject as Cheshire had married a Hollywood film actress, Constance Binney.

There were also various technical flights, such as air tests after maintenance, to be performed. One day Melvin took an aircraft (ED763) to Waddington, just on the other side of Lincoln, to be fitted with 'Two Stage Amber', a blue transparency fitted to the perspex in two of the Lancasters, to be used in conjunction with yellow goggles to simulate moonlight conditions in daytime. Throughout April Melvin managed to fly some thirty-seven hours, but thirty-two of these were in daytime. No doubt his administrative duties interfered, but he must have been eager to get back into flying practice after so long away from operations. By the time of the raid he had accumulated only sixty hours since the squadron was formed, of which twenty-one were at night. On 22 April, Lancaster Type 464, ED887/G (the G showed it must be guarded) was taken on charge by 617 Squadron with the squadron identification AJ-A; this was to be Melvin's aircraft for most of his subsequent flying and the raid. AJ was the two letter aircraft identification code assigned to 617 Squadron; each aircraft had its own additional separate letter, in Melvin's case 'A for Apple'.

One highlight for Melvin during April was to have some time off to act as best man at the wedding of a contemporary from Oxford, Charles McClure, on Saturday 24 April. Charles McClure had also studied law at Trinity and had rowed for the college at Henley. Like Melvin he had joined the RAFVR. He developed a deep interest in aeronautics and became a distin-guished test pilot. Among his exploits was the testing of the carburettor modifications which allowed British fighters to pursue fuel injected Messerschmitts in a dive. Previously, Spitfires and Hurricanes had suffered engine cuts in pushover manoeuvres and Miss Beatrice Shilling, the Royal Aircraft Establishment's carburettor expert, came up with the solution. Charles McClure also did much development flying of early British jet aircraft during the war and later became Professor of

Flight at the College of Aeronautics at Cranfield and a Deputy Lieutenant of Bedfordshire. Charles McClure's bride was Mrs Gay Bevan, the widow of Flight Lieutenant A.W. Bevan who had been killed on a bomber operation in 1942. The wedding took place at the Savoy Chapel in London followed by a small reception at the Inner Temple as Charles McClure's father was a judge.

On 1 May Melvin flew, at low level (200 feet), with Gibson, Whitworth and some of the more experienced members of the squadron to Manston, which is near the eastern corner of Kent and the shallow water at Reculver where trial drops of Upkeep were to take place. These were mostly with inert weapons filled with concrete, although at least one live example was tested. The next two weeks saw Melvin and his crew flying more at night, with numerous 'spotlight runs' and cross-country flights. On 5 May Melvin accompanied Gibson to 5 Group Headquarters at Grantham, returning for some night flying which started with spotlight runs at Uppingham and then via Downham Market to Wainfleet for bombing practice. On this day Lord Trenchard, the 'founding father of the RAF', visited Scampton and addressed the crews.[18] The next day Sir Arthur Harris did likewise; probably Melvin would have been present for these events.

Early in May Gibson had reported that he felt his crews would be able to perform the operation, albeit practice continued at an intense pace. Melvin flew a variety of cross-country and bombing exercises, visiting the lakes at Uppingham, Colchester, Sheffield (Derwent) and the range at Wainfleet. On one flight he had Bill Astell with him and on another Warner Ottley – both were to die on the way to the dams.

On 9 May Melvin and Henry Maudslay flew their aircraft in company to test newly fitted Very High Frequency radio telephone (R/T) sets. These VHF sets had been installed to enable adequate voice communication between aircraft captains in order to control the attack on the dams. Radio silence would be maintained as far as possible and essential communications with 5 Group HQ would be by Wireless/Telegraphy (W/T), the wireless operators sending and receiving messages in Morse code. However it soon became clear that tactical control around the dams would need voice control, thus the fitting of these VHF sets, previously only installed in fighter aircraft.

The Chief Signals Officer at 5 Group HQ in 1943, Wing Commander W.E. Dunn, had been the signals officer for 102 Squadron when Melvin made his two ditchings in the sea in 1940. It was Dunn who had constructed the phoney signal 'posting' Melvin to run a dinghy training school. For Operation Chastise Dunn had devised a system of code words for communication to and from the aircraft. The most significant of these were 'Nigger', to be sent when the Möhne Dam had been breached, and 'Dinghy', Melvin's nickname, when the Eder had been broken. Nigger was the name of Gibson's black Labrador dog, which was to be tragically killed on the day before the raid. The dog ran out of the camp gate and was struck by a car, whose occupants were injured attempting to avoid him. This was undoubtedly a blow to Gibson – it is notable that he did not have the word changed for the operation.

Melvin seems to have taken some passengers flying, perhaps on his own authority. On 9 May he took a Lieutenant Rockwood and a Mr Rodgers, whose identities are unknown to the author, on a night cross-country flight lasting 1 hour and 20 minutes. Possibly one of these was actually his rowing friend Alan Tyser, who, as an Eton College oarsman would have also known Henry Maudslay. Alan confidently asserted that Melvin had taken him for a flight in a Lancaster from a base somewhere in eastern England, and when the author queried this as being unlikely on grounds of security he replied 'Melvin was very determined when he wanted to do something'.[19] Alan recalled how conscious he was of the damage he might do to the inside of the aircraft with his heavy army boots.

On Monday 10 May, Melvin signed a new will, witnessed by his father, Henry, and one of his legal colleagues at a firm of solicitors in Biggleswade, Bedfordshire, where Henry helped out during the war years. On this document Melvin's address was given as that of his father, 117 Fore St, Hertford, a flat above Henry's regular office. It would have been important for Melvin to make this will as a recently married man returning to active service. Guy Gibson had also urged his officers to ensure that their wills were up-to-date – a strong hint that the forthcoming operation would be hazardous.

On 11 May Melvin flew 'Cross country route number 1, returning direct from Colchester' in formation with the aircraft of Maltby and Shannon, with whom he would be flying en route to the dams. From 11 to 13 May various aircraft from 617 flew to Reculver and dropped inert Upkeep weapons towards the beach. It is not recorded whether Melvin was one of these, but as one of the crews chosen to take part in the attack on the principal target, the Möhne Dam, it is likely that he did. Certainly the other flight commander, Henry Maudslay, dropped one on 13 May and the splash from the first bounce damaged his aircraft so badly that it could not be repaired in time for the raid.

Later that day (13 May) a 'dress rehearsal operation' was flown via the lakes at Uppingham and Colchester, which Gibson noted as 'Completely successful'. Section Officer Fay Gillan, one of the intelligence officers at Scampton flew on this exercise with Flight Lieutenant Harold 'Mick' Martin, an Australian with operational experience on Hampdens and Lancasters and noted expert in low flying; she found it a most memorable and exciting experience. All was set for Operation Chastise. Also on 13 May Melvin wrote what was to be his last letter to Priscilla. In this letter he spoke of certain plans he had made which indicated that he expected to go on an operation shortly.[20] He would have also been worried because Priscilla had a medical condition which might soon require surgery.

The Raid

On 15 May the Executive Order for Operation Chastise was issued – the raid to be flown the next night, 16/17 May. The weather forecast was good and the moon (which was full in the period 17-20 May) would rise at 17.00 and set at 04.31 (all times in British Double Summer Time, GMT plus two hours). During the afternoon of 15 May, Barnes Wallis was flown to Scampton, in a Wellington of course, and Melvin was called to a meeting at the Station Commander's house. At this meeting, Melvin, Henry

Maudslay, John Hopgood, who had been selected to be deputy leader for the attack on the Möhne Dam, and Flight Lieutenant Bob Hay, the Australian who was the squadron's bombing leader, were briefed by Wallis and Gibson on the targets, the details of the weapon and its delivery. Such was the level of security that the rest of the aircrews were not told until the pre-raid briefing on 16 May, when models of the Möhne and Sorpe dams were available for inspection, as well as photographs of the other targets. This full briefing, principally by Wallis and Gibson, was very thorough and caused considerable excitement, and possibly some relief that it was not to be the battleship *Tirpitz* . Eighteen months later that ominous ship was sunk by 617 Squadron using a different bomb, also designed by Wallis.

The plan for the operation was that three waves of aircraft would be employed. The first wave of nine aircraft, led by Gibson, would attack the Möhne Dam, then the Eder followed by other targets as directed by wireless from 5 Group HQ if any weapons were still available. This wave would fly in three sections of three aircraft, about ten minutes apart, led by Guy Gibson, Melvin Young and Henry Maudslay. Melvin was to fly accompanied by David Maltby and David Shannon. The second wave would fly, by a different route to confuse enemy defences, to the Sorpe Dam. Indeed, because this route was slightly longer via the islands off north Holland, the second wave actually took off before the first wave. The third wave, also of five aircraft, was to set off later and act as a mobile reserve to be used against such dams as were still unbroken. In all nineteen Type 464 aircraft and their crews were available. The crews of Divall and Wilson had sickness and one aircraft could not be repaired from damage during training.

The Operational Executive Order[21] required that the raid be flown at low level, not above 500 feet, except between Ahlen, the final waypoint, and the target where the leader of each section should climb to 1,000 feet ten miles from the target, presumably to ensure finding the target with certainty. For reasons of surprise, it would be desirable to fly as low as possible to reduce the chance of being seen by the German radar, and thus risk interception by fighters, and to minimize the time of exposure to anti-aircraft guns (flak). The 500 feet limit was an acceptance that it would be essential to identify turning points accurately and the section leaders would have felt particular responsibility to ensure that they kept to the route, which had been devised to avoid known flak locations as far as possible. After the raid Maltby and Shannon commented that Melvin had shown a tendency to fly higher than them, and they had used Aldis signal lamps to warn him to keep low. For his part he would have been feeling a great responsibility to lead his team accurately. It may also be that, with relatively little recent flying, on his first operation in a Lancaster and his first at all for nearly a year, and with a crew with little operational experience, he was more concerned about hitting obstacles on the ground than they were – he had never seen himself as 'the fighter pilot type'!

The hazards of low level operations over enemy territory were such that Harris generally disapproved of using heavy bombers in this role. Operation Chastise was an exception, but the loss on the raid of several aircraft to flak and surface impact supports Harris's general view. It was easy to stray off the route – indeed Gibson missed his turning point at the River Rhine by several miles and had an uncomfortable few minutes getting back on track, being shot at in doing so. One of the second wave aircraft, flown by Geoff Rice, got so low over water in Holland that its Upkeep weapon was torn from the aircraft, albeit Rice got the aircraft home. It should be emphasized that to navigate and fly a Lancaster, which had no power assistance to the controls, for six hours, at very low altitude, at night, over enemy territory, was both physically and mentally exhausting.

So, after the main briefing, the navigators and bomb aimers, who had a vital map reading role at low level, set about marking their maps and preparing their navigation logs, while other crew members relaxed as best they could. Melvin, characteristically, tidied his office. In due course the aircrew had a pre-operational meal. Such was the security that it was only when they were served with bacon and eggs, a delight reserved in wartime for aircrew on operations, that sharp observers such as Fay Gillan deduced that this was for real; no more a practice. No doubt there was the usual fatalistic humour in the vein 'If

you don't come back, can I have your next egg'. Thence to get
kitted up and go out to the waiting aircraft around the perimeter
of the airfield, which was still a large grass aerodrome at this
time; it was due to be laid with hard runways shortly after the
Dams Raid.

At 21.28 the first of the second wave aircraft, AJ-E flown by
Flight Lieutenant Barlow, took off, followed in quick succession
by Munro (AJ-W), Byers (AJ-K) and Rice (AJ-H). None of these
reached their target, the Sorpe Dam. Barlow and Byers were
shot down or crashed en route, Munro was hit by flak and had
to return and, as mentioned before, Geoff Rice had a close call
when his aircraft hit the surface and lost its weapon. Flight
Lieutenant McCarthy DFC RCAF, a very determined American,
was delayed by technical trouble before take-off, transferred to
a spare aircraft (AJ-T) and took off half an hour later – he did
reach the Sorpe and made a skilful and persistent attack, but
only achieved relatively minor damage.

At 21.39 Guy Gibson (AJ-G) took off followed by Hopgood
(AJ-M) and Martin (AJ-P). They formed up in close formation
and came back overhead to set course. At 21.47 Melvin lined A
for Apple up for take-off, David Horsfall applied full power
(3,000 rpm +14 lbs/sq.in. boost) and they rumbled and bounced
across the grass field until flying speed was attained and Melvin
could ease the heavy aircraft off the ground, retract the main
wheels and concentrate on getting the airspeed up and the
climb safely established. Maltby (AJ-J) and Shannon (AJ-L) and
their crews were soon off the ground in turn and the three
aircraft formed up and set course overhead Scampton at 21.58.

The Flight to the Möhne Dam

It is fortunate that the navigation log of Sergeant V. Nicholson,
in David Maltby's AJ-J, has survived and so the progress of
Melvin's section of three aircraft is well described. The first note
in the log on getting airborne was that the IFF (Identify Friend
or Foe) radio was switched on, to ensure that British radar knew
they were indeed 'one of ours'. Within a few minutes they had
settled at a height of 150 feet and were over Woodhall Spa and
shortly after were crossing the north-west coast of the Wash

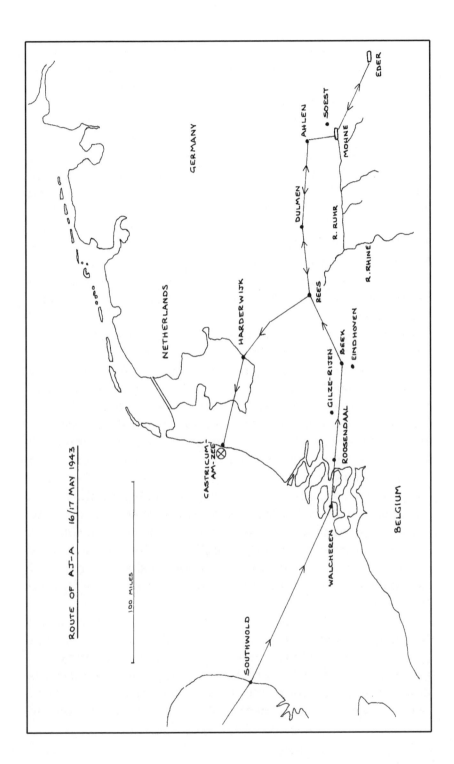

ROUTE OF AJ-A   16/17 MAY 1943

100 MILES

SOUTHWOLD

WALCHEREN

BELGIUM

ROOSENDAAL

EINDHOVEN

BEEK

GILZE-RIJEN

CASTRICUM-AM-ZEE

NETHERLANDS

HARDERWIJK

REES

DULMEN

GERMANY

AHLEN

SOEST

MOHNE

EDER

R. RUHR

R. RHINE

about five miles north-east of Boston. Perhaps they could see the Boston Stump, the tallest parish church tower in Britain, silhouetted against the evening sky, the sun having just set. Over the Wash they let down even lower and tested the spotlights on the water, calibrating the aircraft's pressure altimeters in the process. Soon the south-east coast of the Wash flashed by and they were over Norfolk, not far from the Royal Family's country house at Sandringham. Their route took them via East Dereham (near the USAAF base at Shipdham where Melvin had landed the previous month), Wymondham, Bungay on the River Waveney in Suffolk and on to Southwold with its distinctive lighthouse, where they crossed the English coast at 22.38, having made a ground speed of 175 mph from Scampton with a slight northerly wind helping them along. Thus blacked out Southwold in the twilight was to be the last sight of Britain for Melvin and his crew.

This was a good point for the navigators to take stock of their calculations of the wind, not very strong fortunately, and to restart plotting the aircraft's position from a known point. They were then over the North Sea, with only a very small change of track to their next waypoint at the mouth of the River Scheldt in Holland, between the islands of Schouwen and Walcheren. The IFF could now be switched off – no unnecessary radio transmissions to give away their position to a vigilant enemy. According to Nicholson's log the three aircraft maintained the same average speed (175 mph, ninety-nine miles in thirty-five minutes) and arrived at the Scheldt waypoint at 23.12, on track. As if to demonstrate the difficulty of such navigation, Gibson's section had drifted somewhat south and crossed the heavily defended Walcheren, fortunately without mishap. At this point the bomb aimers armed the self destructive fuses in the Upkeep weapons.

Now began the difficult task of flying low over enemy territory and finding the way while avoiding obstacles such as power lines and pylons – both the front gunner and the bomb aimer had a literally vital role in looking out for such hazards and warning the pilot to pull up in good time. The route had been chosen with easily identifiable waypoints and reasonably short distances between them, avoiding known flak concentrations as far as possible. As they flew in over the eastern arm of the Scheldt there were good coast line features to confirm that they were on track to the next waypoint at the small town of Roosendaal, which is a short distance inland from the estuary and distinguished by a railway junction. They had to take some evasive action from flak on this leg of the route, and the ground speed declined to 162 mph, perhaps due to a combination of this manoeuvring and an increasing easterly component in the wind.

Having passed Roosendaal at 23.25 the route required a small heading change to the left to pass south of Breda and Tilburg and pick up the helpful line feature of the Wilhelmina Canal. This feature would guide them clear of the heavily defended aerodromes at Gilze-Rijen (between Breda and Tilburg) on their left and Eindhoven on the right. It was vitally important to avoid these airfields as was to be shown, tragically, later that night when one of the third wave aircraft, AJ-S, flown by Pilot Officer Lewis Burpee DFM, RCAF, strayed over Gilze-Rijen and was brought down by the defences.

Eindhoven was the location of the important Philips radio factory which had been pressed into service for the Germans and had been the target for the daring low-level daylight raid, Operation Oyster, by the medium bombers – Bostons and Mosquitos – of 2 Group on 6 December 1942. This raid had achieved much damage but at a cost of twelve of the seventy-eight attacking aircraft. The defences had been strong then and could be expected to be even more dangerous five months on. Beyond Eindhoven the canal met another at right angles by a village called Beek and this made a prominent waypoint. Melvin's section arrived at Beek at 23.42 and Nicholson observed that 'Leader turned soon' – perhaps Melvin was a bit higher than the others to be sure of seeing the turning point and anticipated the turn, of some 20 degrees left, towards the next waypoint at Rees on the River Rhine which they reached at 23.56.

Melvin's section was now averaging about 170 mph ground speed. Nicholson recorded that the electronic navigational aid

GEE was 'jammed something chronic' at this time. GEE was a 'hyperbolic' area navigation system, similar to the later Decca and LORAN systems, which sent signals from three transmitters in England. These signals could be plotted by the navigators on special charts to give a reasonably accurate fix of position. However, like all such radio aids the enemy could be relied on to try to interfere with the signals. Most of the navigators on the raid had trouble with GEE, except Knight's navigator, Hobday; perhaps he was particularly adept at operating the quite complex receiver.

From Rees they flew almost due east to a group of lakes near Dulmen. On this leg they met some well-directed flak which again caused them to take evasive action. Although Melvin and his section got through this area successfully, Henry Maudslay's group was less fortunate. Bill Astell's aircraft (AJ-B) fell someway behind the others and shortly afterwards, at 00.15, hit a power pylon and crashed near Marbeck, three miles south of Borken. The Upkeep broke away from the rest of the wreckage and careered on across the fields before its self-destruct fuse set it off, making a large crater. This event is prominent in the folk memory of the area and is commemorated in a small museum in a nearby village. Astell, who had survived the desert war by skill and courage, had now run out of luck. Another member of Melvin's 'A' Flight, Robert Barlow in AJ-E, had already crashed just east of Rees having hit high tension wires. Barlow's weapon did not explode and was recovered and analysed by the Germans. Barlow was the first of the second wave which had followed a more northerly route before turning at Rees. This aircraft crashed at 23.50 just minutes before Melvin passed nearby. The hazards of low flying were starting to take their toll.

Having reached the Dulmen waypoint at 00.09 they turned 15 degrees right to head for Ahlen which had a conspicuous railway line. Ahlen was successfully identified at 00.20 and they turned right again onto a south-south-easterly heading to pass between the small towns of Werl and Soest, having to take more evasive action. Coming now into somewhat more hilly country and approaching the Möhne Melvin would have climbed AJ-A to make sure he could see the lake in good time. It was now

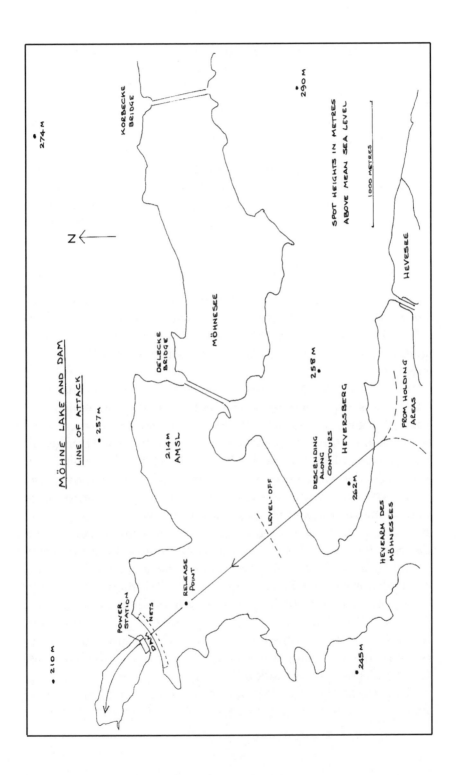

MÖHNE LAKE AND DAM

LINE OF ATTACK

SPOT HEIGHTS IN METRES
ABOVE MEAN SEA LEVEL

1000 METRES

• 274 M

KORBECKE BRIDGE

• 290 M

• 257M

• 210 M

DELECKE BRIDGE

MÖHNESEE

214 M AMSL

258 M

HEVERSBERG

DESCENDING ALONG CONTOURS

262M

LEVEL-OFF

FROM HOLDING AREAS

HEVESEE

POWER STATION

DAM

NETS

RELEASE POINT

HEVEARM DES MÖHNESEES

• 245 M

00.26, although Shannon arrived slightly after the other two and was shot at by the defences for his trouble. Nicholson's log records that they now switched on their VHF radio sets and started circling in pre-arranged locations, and commented that the 'flak [was] none too light'. They had arrived at the principal target. In Gibson's words:

> As we came over the hill, we saw the Möhne Lake. Then we saw the dam itself. In that light it looked squat and heavy and unconquerable; it looked grey and solid in the moonlight as though it were part of the countryside itself and just as immovable.[22]

The Attack on the Möhne Dam

The scene was now set for the most famous and ingenious attack in the history of the RAF – requiring a degree of precision not to be repeated until the advent of sophisticated electronic guidance systems. It was conducted with remarkable skill and great courage.

The Möhne lake (Möhnesee) is aligned east-west and has two main arms separated by a wooded peninsula on which the highest point is called the Heversberg. The larger, northern arm is fed by the Möhne River and is crossed by two road bridges at the villages of Delecke and Korbecke. The shorter, southern arm (Hevearm des Möhnesees on the map) is fed by a small river, the Heve. The dam, which is some 650 metres long, 30 metres high and 30 metres thick at the base, lies at the north-west corner of the lake. It is aligned roughly north-east to south-west, and to attack it at right angles to its centre point required the aircraft to fly in on a heading of approximately 330 degrees (30 degrees west of north). The Heversberg rises to 262 metres (860 feet) above sea level and the lake surface, when full, is at 214 metres (700 feet). The dam was defended by a dozen quick firing anti-aircraft (flak) guns, some on the towers of the dam and some in the surrounding country. Just below the air face of the dam was a hydroelectric power station.

The geography of the dam and the performance of the aircraft made it necessary to attack by lining up over the Hevearm, diving and skimming down the Heversburg peninsula just above the trees to gain the necessary speed (220 mph) to release the weapon. Indeed Gibson's account[23] tells us that his bomb aimer warned him: 'You're going to hit those trees.' However it was indeed necessary to get down to the bombing height as early as possible in the run – the author's calculations show that if the aircraft was levelled off 1,650 yards from the dam (the shore is only 1,900 yards out), then at 220 mph there would be only eleven seconds before reaching the release point at 450 yards; not much time, but just enough for a well-trained, determined crew. In this short time the height had to be settled at 60 feet and the line adjusted to aim at the centre of the dam, with the wings level. A firm grip on the control wheel would have been needed even if the adrenalin was not pumping – Melvin's rowing muscles would now be a bonus.

The engine throttles would have been adjusted by the flight engineer to maintain the speed gained in the dive. In addition to the noise and vibration from the engines and propellers, high enough anyway, there would have been the added vibration, with a different frequency and amplitude, of the weapon rotating at 500 rpm as it needed to be run up ten minutes before the attack. Although the weapons were balanced as well as possible, it was reported that they did cause a noticeable vibration.

Some books on the raid have shown the line of attack as being along the northern arm of the lake, followed by a right turn, which would have to be through at least 70 degrees, to line up towards the dam. The author's calculations have shown that this would have required a bank angle of approximately 50 degrees, more or less depending on assumptions, which, with a Lancaster wingspan of 102 feet, would result in the wing tip being only twenty feet above the water. Experienced pilots are unlikely to have contemplated this sort of semi-aerobatic manoeuvre in the dark – the merest sideslip would have put the wing in the water. After the turn there would only be about three to five seconds left to get the all important height, line and level attitude. Also the associated load factor ('g' loading) in the turn would be over 1.5g and this would result in a loss of speed.

Inspection of the briefing model for the Möhne, on display at the Imperial War Museum, confirms, in the author's opinion, that the only practical option would have been to descend straight over the Heversberg.

On arrival at the Möhne, Gibson circled the lake and dam to 'size it up' and said over the radio that 'he liked the look of it'. At this time, 00.26, Young's section arrived. The tactic was to be that Gibson would attack first with the others orbiting at low altitude in agreed positions nearby. They would to come in to attack in turn at the leader's command – he would call them on VHF using the call-sign 'Cooler', with a number denoting their position in the order of action – thus AJ-A would be 'Cooler 4'. Gibson reminded Hopgood to take over from him should he be knocked out of the action. At 00.28 Guy Gibson made the first attack in the face of significant anti-aircraft fire. His weapon bounced three times, sank and exploded sending up a column of water to about 1,000 feet. When the lake settled it could be seen that the dam was unbroken. A coded signal was sent by Gibson's wireless operator to 5 Group HQ, where Harris, Cochrane and Wallis were waiting expectantly, reporting that the 'mine' had exploded without breaching the dam. Subsequent analysis supports this report that this weapon may have stopped and sunk just short of the dam, possibly having hit and broken the anti-torpedo nets thus clearing the way for following weapons.

Next Hopgood was called in to attack, just as Maudslay and Knight arrived at 00.32. It seems likely that Hopgood's aircraft had been hit by flak on the flight to the Möhne and that Hopgood himself had been injured. Undeterred he made his run at the dam but was hit again and his aircraft fatally damaged, catching fire and eventually exploding. Thus it seems, not surprisingly, that the crew had difficulty getting all the necessary conditions right for the release. However the bomb aimer, realizing the aircraft was doomed, released the weapon anyway, too late, and it bounced over the dam and fell on the power station below. It was destroyed in a blinding flash when the delayed action fuse detonated the high explosive, at about the time that the aircraft crashed some six kilometres from the dam where it burned fiercely throughout the rest of the action. With notable heroism, which received no official recognition later, Hopgood climbed the aircraft as high as he could, and said to his crew 'For Christ's sake get out'. Two of them, the bomb aimer Flight Sergeant J.W. Fraser, RCAF and the rear gunner Pilot Officer A.F. Burcher, DFM, RAAF, did manage to escape despite the low altitude. Flight Lieutenant John Vere Hopgood, from Seaford in Sussex, already held the DFC and Bar and was only 21 years old. He had prophesied to Shannon just before take-off: 'I think this is going to be a tough one, and I don't think I'm coming back, Dave.'[24]

Next it was the turn of Flight Lieutenant Harold B. 'Mick' Martin DFC, an Australian who had joined the RAF. At 00.38 he made his run. This time Gibson flew in somewhat ahead of Martin and to his right, to distract the German defences and let his own gunners engage them. Both aircraft survived the flak, although Martin's aircraft was hit but not badly damaged. Martin's bomb aimer was Flight Lieutenant R.C. 'Bob' Hay, DFC, RAAF whose experience had led to his being made the squadron bombing leader. A huge explosion and column of water resulted from this weapon, such that the rear gunner could not see how many bounces had been achieved. Unfortunately this weapon had veered off to the left and exploded near the southern shore of the lake. The defenders were shaken and drenched but the dam was still there. The most likely explanation was that the Upkeep had met the water slightly off level and thus did not bounce straight. Wallis was aware that the cylindrical design was vulnerable to this effect, but had been forced to adopt this design after unsuccessful experiments with a spherical shape.

Then at 00.43 Melvin and his crew made their attempt. Melvin would have climbed AJ-A from its holding orbit to a height which practice had told him would be enough to achieve 220 mph after a shallow dive, with the weapon on. He visually lined up with the centre of the dam and pushed the nose down to gain speed, following the contours of the Heversberg peninsula as closely as he dared. He may have trimmed the elevator to ease some of his forward push on the control wheel, but would probably have left some nose-up trim in case he needed to go around or was himself hit, in which case the aircraft would climb and give the crew some chance of survival. Meanwhile Larry Nichols, the wireless operator, had checked that the weapon was rotating at 500 rpm -it would probably have been set running soon after they reached the Möhne. Charles Roberts, the navigator, had switched on the spotlights and positioned himself by the starboard blister in the cockpit canopy in order to give Melvin up/down guidance over the water surface. David Horsfall, the flight engineer, controlled the engine throttles and kept a close watch on the airspeed indicator, aiming to have the speed at 220 mph as they levelled over the lake and pushing the levers forward as necessary to maintain that speed. The air gunners, Gordon Yeo and Wilfred Ibbotson, prepared to engage the defences – all the squadron guns were loaded with tracer ammunition the better to assess their aim and, hopefully, frighten the enemy.

Gibson, whose leadership throughout can only be described as heroic, was now flying on the air side of the dam to distract the enemy gunners and Martin flew in alongside AJ-A to draw some of the flak. We can only conjecture what it was like for Melvin as they rushed down over the trees and he levelled off quickly as near to 60 feet as he could judge, listening for Roberts' voice to guide him up or down, and for Vincent MacCausland, lying in the bomb aimer's position, calling, if necessary, for slight adjustments in heading, which needed to be made with firm but smooth pressure on the rudders, with a bit of aileron to ensure that the wings stayed level. Meanwhile Gordon Yeo was shooting at the guns on the dam, some of which would have been returning his fire. Larry Nichols was prepared to fire a red Very flare when they had dropped the weapon and crossed the dam. The moon was behind the aircraft, thus silhouetting them for the flak gunners. And all this happened very fast – only about ten seconds from levelling off over the water until Vincent MacCausland pressed the release and their Upkeep fell away and started its career towards the dam.

After its release the weapon fell further behind the aircraft with each bounce and the rear gunner could see the plumes of spray. Gibson recorded that Young's weapon made 'three good bounces and contact' [with the dam]. It sank to its preset depth and exploded against the dam wall as Wallis had predicted. Another huge column of water rose and a shock wave could be seen rippling through the lake. Melvin glanced back and thought he must have broken it – in fact later analysis indicated that the dam was now beginning to break but it did not collapse immediately. And so Nichols sent a wireless signal to HQ saying they had hit the dam but it was unbroken; the mood at 5 Group HQ was becoming despondent.

It was now David Maltby's turn to attack in AJ-J at 00.49. Gibson and Martin orbited on the water side of the dam, engaging the flak positions, some of which had now been silenced, to take the heat off AJ-J. As Maltby raced in he saw that 'the crown of the wall was already crumbling ...a tremendous amount of debris on the top...a breach in the centre of the dam'. With admirable presence of mind in the time available he adjusted his line slightly left and his weapon was released. It bounced four times, struck the dam, sank and exploded. In the initial confusion of flak and water it was not immediately obvious that the dam was now broken and Gibson called Shannon to get ready, but was soon able to tell him to hold off. When the spray had subsided Gibson had been able to see that a great gap, some 150 metres long, had appeared in the dam and a torrent of water surged down the valley below – 'looking like stirred porridge in the moonlight'. There followed a lot of excited calls on the R/T – Maltby's navigator, Nicholson, recorded 'Bomb Dropped Wizard' in his log. Thus about forty minutes after Gibson had reached the Möhne, the code word 'Nigger' was transmitted by Gibson's wireless operator, at 00.56. This was received and decoded by Wing Commander Dunn at 5 Group HQ and the excitement there equalled that over the Möhne. Wallis danced for joy and Harris was delighted to find his scepticism misplaced.

On to the Eder

There were now only three aircraft of the first wave armed with Upkeep; AJ-Z (Maudslay), AJ-L (Shannon) and AJ-N (Knight).

Gibson called Astell, but to no avail; unknown to the others he and his crew had died just before Gibson had arrived at the Möhne. Conscious of the time, Gibson sent Martin and Maltby home and, with Melvin as his deputy, led the three armed aircraft towards the Eder Dam. This was a flight of about fifteen minutes over increasingly hilly country, with the pilots trying to keep down in the valleys as much as possible. Now well past midnight some mist was beginning to form under the clear skies. The Edersee (Ederstausee on some maps) is a very long lake with more than one arm and Shannon at least found it difficult to find the dam, until Gibson fired a Very light over it.

The Eder Dam was not defended by guns, but it was in very difficult terrain. It soon became clear that the only way to get down to the lake was by descending along a valley from beside the *Schloss* (Castle) at Waldeck, about two miles north of the dam on the other side of the lake. The descent from the castle was not directly towards the dam and there was another spur of land, shown on some maps as the Hammerberg, protruding into the lake on the ideal line towards the centre of the dam. It is not clear just what tactics each pilot chose to approach it. Probably a descending turn towards the dam was started as soon as they were clear of the valley onto the best line they could make. There would then be very little time to get down and stabilized at 60 feet and 220 mph. Even then a line aimed at right angles to the centre of the dam was not feasible, possibly 25 degrees off, and this explains why the breach, when it was finally achieved, was towards the southern end of the dam.

It was going to take the three attacking aircraft eleven attempts to launch three weapons. To add insult to injury, on passing over the dam there is a significant mountain, the Michelskopf, directly ahead, requiring a climbing turn to avoid it. This would have been especially daunting when overshooting with the weapon still onboard – no doubt the Merlin engines were called on for emergency power, 'through the gate'. Melvin's role at the Eder was a watching brief, ready to take over from Gibson if necessary; if, for instance, Gibson had technical trouble with the VHF radio. Arguably this was the worst job of the night – very tense and hoping they would succeed and allow everyone to be on the way home before the dawn.

Gibson ordered Shannon to make the first attack. It is best described in Dave Shannon's own words:[25]

> The Eder was a bugger of a job....I was first to go; I tried three times to get a 'spot on' approach but was never satisfied. To get out of the valley after crossing the dam wall we had to put on full throttle and do a steep climbing turn to avoid a vast rock face. My exit with a 9000lb bomb revolving at 500rpm was bloody hairy. Then Gibson told us to take a breather and Henry Maudslay went in.

Henry Maudslay and his crew made two runs without feeling able to release their weapon. Then Shannon tried again and after two more unsuccessful attempts launched his Upkeep at 01.39. It bounced twice, hit the water face of the dam and sank, followed by the now expected explosion sending a column of water up to a great height. The dam did not immediately fall, but it was no doubt weakened. Then Henry Maudslay made another attempt and this time released the weapon, but just too late – it hit the parapet of the dam at high velocity and this impact caused the bomb to detonate spontaneously. Fortunately the aircraft had already passed the dam but, no doubt, felt the blast. Maudslay, asked on the radio if he was alright, was heard to reply, faintly 'I think so'. The others did not see him again, but he seems to have struggled with a probably damaged aircraft and attempted to get home, only to be shot down near the German-Dutch border.

Now only Les Knight in AJ-N had a weapon. He made two attempts and on the second got into a good position and released the Upkeep at 01.52. It bounced three times and hit the dam to the right of centre. Gibson described this attack:

> ..we were flying above him, and about 400 yards to the right, and saw his mine hit the water. We saw where it sank. We saw the tremendous earthquake which shook the base of the dam, and then, as if a gigantic hand had punched a hole through cardboard, the whole thing collapsed.

No doubt with great relief, Melvin's nick-name 'Dinghy' was transmitted back to 5 Group HQ, to be received with yet more celebration. Over the Eder it was time to get home.

While all this was going on at the Möhne and the Eder Dams, it should not be forgotten that other 617 Squadron pilots were making heroic attempts elsewhere. McCarthy and Brown made valiant attacks on the Sorpe, albeit frustrated by the unsuitability of Upkeep for that type of dam. Townsend launched a weapon unsuccessfully at another dam, late in the night, and had to race the dawn home crossing Holland in daylight.

Flight back to Disaster

The four aircraft over the Eder now had a strong incentive to get home safely and as quickly as possible. Three return routes had been specified in the operational order; all involved retracing the route via the Möhne Dam, Ahlen and the lakes at Dulmen. From Dulmen there was some choice, but all routes involved crossing the Ijsselmeer (Zuider Zee) and the Helder peninsula in north Holland. Melvin and Guy Gibson seem to have chosen the most southerly route which continued back to the same crossing point on the Rhine at Rees, then north-west to near Harderwijk on the Ijsselmeer, across that stretch of water via the picturesque island village of Marken and on to leave the Dutch North Sea coast at a known 'gap' in the defences near Egmond. If, as seems likely, they set course from the Eder at approximately 01.55, and given that Melvin in AJ-A seems to have reached the North Sea in a few minutes over one hour, he must have averaged a speed of about 215 mph – full throttle all the way and as low as possible.

Gibson recorded that as they passed the Möhnesee the river below was several times its normal width and the level of water in the lake had fallen considerably – water was still flowing through the breach when, a few hours later, a photo-reconnaissance Spitfire took the now famous 'morning after' pictures. At Rees, on the Rhine, they would have turned north-west and passed over Emmerich close to the Dutch-German border at about the same time as Henry Maudslay was shot down near there, having struggled that far with his damaged aircraft flying rather slower. The route then took them between Arnhem and Apeldoorn and on towards Harderwijk.

As Melvin and his crew raced across the Ijsselmeer, the island of Marken would have given them a line that would, in turn, have led them to the Noordhollandskanal which points west-north-west towards the coast at Egmond, where they would hopefully be far enough away from the heavy defences around IJmuiden, a busy harbour and E-boat base. The country is very flat but there is a ridge of dunes just inland of the coast. Folk memory in that part of north Holland[26] tells of a tower on the ridge near Egmond that was a good marker for low flying pilots – if they crossed near it the guns north of IJmuiden at Castricum-aan-Zee would be hard put to hit them. There was also a hazard from flak at an aerodrome near Bergen a short way to the north. The general advice was to cross the coast as fast and as low as possible. Two of the pilots, Gibson and Shannon, climbed quite high, 800 feet according to Shannon, a few miles before the coast and crossed it in a full throttle dive, judging the flight path to give the guns the least chance of success.

Sadly, in the case of Melvin Young and his crew the guns were successful. At 02.58 gunners at Castricum-aan-Zee reported shooting down an aircraft they took to be a Halifax, but it almost certainly was Melvin's Lancaster and several batteries also reported firing at it. AJ-A crashed into the sea and all its crew were killed. Over the North Sea, Guy Gibson called Melvin on the radio…there was no reply.

It will never be known whether Melvin crossed the coast too high, or too near IJmuiden – his inexperienced navigator, Charles Roberts, aided by Vincent MacCausland map reading in the nose of the aircraft, seems to have done an admirable job of helping the captain find the way previously. Melvin had demonstrated at the Möhne Dam that he had become a very accomplished pilot, and had trained his crew well. Nonetheless, one hit with a high explosive shell had a good chance of destroying an aircraft, and so it was. Whatever the reason, their luck had deserted them at the last hurdle and thus ended their historic and heroic last night.

The surviving eleven Type 464 Provisioning Lancasters from Operation Chastise landed back at Scampton between 03.11 and 06.15 to be greeted and congratulated by Harris, Wallis and many others. Eight aircraft had been lost and fifty-three flyers had died. Much damage had been done to the enemy and the Royal Air Force's fame was enhanced forever.

Notes
1. National Archives Air 29/613.
2. ibid.
3. Records of Robert Owen, official historian to 617 Squadron Aircrew Association.
4. Miss Lettice Curtis.
5. National Archives AIR 14/595.
6. *Wellington Wings*, F.R. Chappell.
7. Enemy Coast Ahead, Guy P. Gibson
8. Private correspondence with author.
9. Private correspondence.
10. Private correspondence.
11. Fred Sutherland.
12. Pilot Officer I. Whittaker, flight engineer.
13. National Archives AIR14/2036.
14. Ref. Log of Sergeant Nicholson, Maltby's navigator.
15. National Archives AIR 14/2088.
16. National Archives AIR 14/2036.
17. *The Dambusters Raid*, John Sweetman.
18. National Archives AIR 27/2128, 617 Squadron ORB.
19. Private correspondence.
20. Letter from Hobart Rawson to Father Chalmers, 12 June 1943.
21. National Archives AIR 14/2088.
22. Gibson, op. cit.
23. ibid.
24. *There Shall Be Wings*, Max Arthur, 1993.
25. ibid.
26. Author's conversations with Mr Jaap Kroon.

Chapter 10

Afterwards

The news of the Dams' raid was reported by the BBC on 17 May and splashed across all the British newspapers on 18 May, with that most famous of photo-reconnaissance pictures – taken by a Spitfire just hours afterwards – showing the large breach in the Möhne Dam with the water still clearly flowing through. The story also made news across the Atlantic, as it was intended to do, featuring, *inter alia*, in *TIME* on 31 May. Indeed Guy Gibson was sent on a tour of North America to meet the people and tell the story. His words appeared in serious journals such as *The Atlantic Report* (Cracking the German Dams, Wing Commander Guy P Gibson, December 1943).

Meanwhile, in Germany, after initial anguish, enormous efforts were made to rebuild the Möhne Dam – it was ready again by autumn but at the price of diverting many thousands of workers from tasks such as building the defences along the Atlantic Coast.

During Gibson's tour, in Calgary, he met one Robert Young, a 20 year old trainee RAF wireless operator from California. Robert was the 'would be adopted brother' who lived with Fannie and had taken the Young name; unlike Dodd, he was never formally adopted by Henry and Fannie and was one of the causes of the rift between them. Gibson gave him some words of encouragement, stressing the value of all members of a bomber crew. Whereas Dodd Young, who was properly adopted, became a valued member of the Rowan family business in Los Angeles, Robert does not seem to have become 'one of the family' and worked in various capacities in the motion picture industry.

Immediately after the raid it was Gibson's duty to write to the next of kin of the fifty-six men who had not returned from the raid, to tell them that their loved ones were missing, and to express hope that they had survived and would be reported as prisoners of war. In fact only three had survived. Harry Humphries, the 617 Squadron Adjutant, records in his book *Living With Heroes* that telegrams were sent immediately and that he and Gibson rapidly organized all the paperwork which ensued, especially the letters. Guy Gibson took this duty very seriously and wrote all the letters personally over the next few days.

In Melvin's case he had nominated his father as next-of-kin. He did not wish Priscilla immediately to receive news that he had gone missing, preferring his father to use his judgement. He had also asked his father to send news to the USA via Father Chalmers at Kent School, so that he in turn could break it carefully via Priscilla's father, Hobart Rawson. Gibson's letter to Henry Young, dated on what would have been Melvin's 28th birthday, 20 May 1943, reads:

My dear Mr Young,

It is with deep regret that I write to confirm my telegram advising you that your son, Squadron Leader Henry Melvin Young D.F.C., is missing as a result of operations.

Squadron Leader Young was a great personal friend of mine and was himself largely responsible for the success of this operation. He was deputy leader of this raid and I watched him drop his load in exactly the right position with great precision. Afterwards we led the raid on the Eder dam and he and I flew on the return journey back to base. Somewhere, however, between the target and the enemy coast he ran into trouble and has not returned.

If as is possible your son was able to abandon his aircraft and land safely in enemy territory, news should reach you direct from the International Red Cross Committee within the next six weeks. Please accept my sincere sympathy during this anxious period of waiting.

I have arranged for his personal effects to be taken care of by the Committee of Adjustment Officer and these will be forwarded to you through the normal channels in due course.

If there is any way in which I can help you please let me know.

Yours sincerely

(Signed by Guy Gibson)

A total of thirty-three awards were made to surviving aircrew, including Gibson's Victoria Cross – possibly a record for one unit accomplishing one operation. Five of the pilots were awarded the next most distinguished award for gallantry, the Distinguished Service Order (DSO). Had they survived, the two flight commanders, Melvin Young and Henry Maudslay, would undoubtedly have received the DSO but, unlike the VC, such awards are not made posthumously.

As May wore on the North Sea gave up the bodies of Melvin and his crew. They were washed ashore by the tides some miles to the north of where they crashed and are buried in the General Cemetery of the nearest small town, Bergen, North Holland. Five of them are buried side by side; Melvin's grave is in the centre of this group, with Vincent MacCausland and Gordon Yeo on his right and David Horsfall and Wilfred Ibbotson to his left. The bodies of Charles Roberts and Lawrence Nichols were recovered later and are buried separately, but nearby. Altogether some 250 Allied airmen are buried in this cemetery and all their names are recorded on a bell in the carillon in the town. There is also a small building at the entrance to the cemetery which displays interesting memorabilia – the Dambuster crew have prominence. When the author and his wife visited the cemetery in April 2006, there were fresh flowers by each grave of Melvin's crew, complementing the pleasant and dignified planting which is a feature of all Commonwealth War Grave Commission cemeteries.

Among German records is a photograph of the wreckage of a Lancaster on the beach near Bergen from the same period – it is not certain that this was A-JA but it seems likely that it was.

There followed an agonizing period of uncertainty for Melvin's family, especially Priscilla. By a tragic coincidence Priscilla was admitted to hospital in New York for a hysterectomy before she had received his last letter or the news that he was missing. It was to be a most distressing time for a woman of 34 to lose both her husband and the prospect of having children. Priscilla was driven from New York to Ravenscroft on Monday 7 June by her mother and brother, and spent several days recuperating in bed. During that week her family had given her Melvin's last letter because she was fretting at not having received one for several weeks, but this 'broke her up completely' and she was unable to come down for meals until the weekend.[1] Mrs Rawson had been in communication with the 'Air Vice Marshal in Washington', but 'they could give no definite news'.

The following Monday, 14 June, Priscilla received a copy of Guy Gibson's letter to Henry Young. It gave:

> ...the clearest account we have of Melvin. It is some satisfaction to us all to know that he had accomplished his mission successfully before he was forced down. Now we can only hope that we may receive news within the next month that he landed safely and is now a prisoner.[2]

It was not until August that the family finally received confirmation that Melvin had been killed and was buried in Holland. This sad news at least enabled them, on both sides of the Atlantic, to take steps to tidy up his affairs and arrange memorial services. In Connecticut the Rawsons asked Kent School if a service in memory of Melvin could be held in October. Priscilla needed some time to gain her strength and adjust to her loss and her parents were in the process of moving from their apartment in New York to retirement at Ravenscroft Farm. So it was arranged that a service was held in the Kent School Chapel on Sunday evening, 17 October at 6 p.m. The notice advised of a train leaving Grand Central Terminal (New York) at 2.25 p.m. which could be met at Pawling at 4.35, where transport to the school would be waiting – a return train would leave Kent at 7.12 allowing attendees time to have a brief supper.

The school newspaper, *Kent News*, recorded that several

alumni of the school faculty, who remembered Melvin, served at the service, namely Ted Evans, Bill Nadal, Bill and Bob Worthington, Oliver Butterworth, Kent Smith and Robert Morehouse. The next day Clementine Rawson wrote to Father Chalmers to thank him for a:

...perfect service for Melvin. We all just loved it. I don't think that Priscilla and I have had any bitterness of spirit but if we had had it would be gone now.

Hobart Rawson had also written to Father Sill to thank him for:

...the beautiful memorial service for Melvin this afternoon. It recalled to me very vividly the Sunday afternoon services we used to attend when the chapel was first opened and our boys were still in school. The boys always enter into the service so wholeheartedly and sing the hymns with such gusto that it is most impressive. I am sure the service was just what Melvin would have wished it to be.

Hobart Rawson's reference to 'when our boys were in school' shows how much Melvin had become a part of their family. In due course the Rawsons endowed the conversion of a room in the original farm building of Kent School, Old Main, to be called the 'Melvin Young Room' – it is still at the heart of the admissions department of the school.

In the USA, death notices for Melvin appeared in the *New York Times*, the *New York Herald Tribune*, the *Boston Herald*, the *New Milford Times* and a Cincinnati paper, for the benefit of that branch of the Rawson family. In Britain *The Times* carried an obituary on 30 November 1943, giving a brief outline of his education and career; it mentioned that he was the only son of Mr H.G.M. Young of Hertford and Mrs Young of Pasadena, California and that he was married to Priscilla, only daughter of Mr and Mrs Hobart Rawson of Ravenscroft Farm, Kent, Connecticut.

A few weeks later, on Monday 20 December, a joint memorial service was held for Melvin and his good friend Con Cherry, who had died when HMS *Welshman* was sunk on 1 February 1943. The service was held at 2 p.m. in St Margaret,

Westminster, appropriately for two students from Westminster School. After Psalm 121 and the lesson from Wisdom III, 1-9,[3] came Sir Cecil Spring Rice's famous, and entirely appropriate, hymn:

> 'I vow to thee, my Country, all earthly things above,
> Entire and whole and perfect, the service of my love;
> The love that asks no question, the love that stands the test,
> That lays upon the Altar the dearest and the best....
> ...And soul by soul and silently her shining bounds increase,
> And her ways are ways of gentleness and all her paths are peace.'

Then, after prayers, the service ended with the hymn:

> Jesus lives! thy terrors now
> Can, O death, no more appal us;

followed by the benediction.

Canon A.C. Don and the Revd G.A. Ellison (Chaplain RNVR) officiated.

Relatives and others present included:

> Mrs Cherry (widow), Mr E.H. Cherry (father), Mr H.G.M. Young (father), Miss Angela Young, Miss M.A. Young (sisters), Miss Gearing ('Aunt Bert', Melvin's devoted godmother, also representing Mrs Young, widow), Miss Bridget Nendick (Melvin's goddaughter), representatives of the Leander Club and Westminster School, Captain D. Friedberger (HMS *Welshman*), Mrs Reginald Martin (Aunt Bert's sister Ethel), Mr G.O. Nickalls (rowing coach to the 1938 Oxford boat), Alan Tyser, and Mr M. Hillary (father of Richard Hillary, author of *The Last Enemy* and member of the 1938 Trinity Head of the River crew).

Of the people attending the memorial service, none was more affected than Melvin's devoted godmother, Miss Alberta Wake Gearing, 'Aunt Bert', who had followed his career throughout his life and kept a room for him in her apartment as if he were a son. So, with the help of Henry Young and Philip Landon, she set up a bursary in Melvin's memory at Trinity College. The award of this bursary was to be at the college's discretion but preference would be given to students who had served in the RAF, or the sons of RAF veterans or casualties. The first beneficiary was David Mitchell who had been selected for pilot training by the RAF but who had found that he and the air force were in mutual agreement that he was not pilot material. Thus it was with some trepidation when he arrived at Trinity that he found himself invited to dinner at the Mitre Hotel in Oxford by Miss Gearing and her sister. Would they approve of him? He found, to his consternation, that these ladies were formally dressed in the style of a previous generation and on first sight looked quite daunting. His very entertaining account of his RAF career and what turned out to be a congenial dinner is in the Trinity archives. The bursary continued to be awarded for some years, eventually being overtaken by changes in the funding available to students at Oxford.

In January 1944 Melvin's last will, dated 10 May 1943, a week before his death, was granted probate with his father, Henry, as sole executor. Melvin's estate amounted to £4,433, 18 shillings and 10 pence – not a fortune but a substantial sum which would have been enough to buy a comfortable house at that time. He made the following bequests:

> To Trinity College Oxford, the sum of Twenty Pounds for the purchase of silver tankards, also my collection of books on rowing, my racing sculling boat and pair, my oars and sculls.
>
> To Leander Club, Ten Pounds
>
> To the Westminster School Society £50 (fifty pounds)
>
> To the Kent School U.S.A. Fifty pounds[4]
>
> To the Westminster & Keystone Lodge No. 10 of Free & Accepted Masons £25 (twenty five pounds) for the purchase of a piece of silver.[5]

To my father I give all the sums from my policy of life insurance with the London Life Association.

To my wife Priscilla I give the £2,000 4% Funding Loan Stock standing in my name which was a wedding present, also such furniture now in California with my mother, formerly hers and my father's which they have given me and also such of my chattels as she may desire. I make no greater provision for her as she has an ample income of her own.

I devise and bequeath all the residue of my estate to my father should he survive me for one year but should he not do so then I give all the residue to my wife.

Thus Henry Young had the task, not uncommon during the war, of acting as executor of his son's estate. Henry would have been guided by Melvin's letter, written at the start of the war and to be opened on his death. In that letter Melvin also mentions the life insurance policy, acknowledging that Henry had paid the premiums '...and [you] have made so many sacrifices for me'. Melvin also remembered his sisters Punkie (Mary) and Angela in this letter, albeit nearly four years had passed by the time his will was written and he was then married and their own careers were developing. The letter ends:

Don't be sad that I am dead: I am at last happy...with all my love from your devoted son ..Melvin

Also early in 1944 Priscilla received Melvin's personal effects, including a 'goodbye', handwritten letter from him. She was just about to leave Ravenscroft for Boston where she had found a job which would take her mind off her loss. Fortunately the letter came while she was still at home with her mother. Clementine Rawson recorded that:

...it was the most beautiful letter full of love, hope and happiness – the wedding was a success.

Four months later, on Tuesday 13 June, Priscilla was in Washington to receive the Bar to Melvin's DFC from the hands of the British Ambassador, Lord Halifax, whom Melvin had heard speak at Oxford in 1940. The ceremony was held in the ballroom of the embassy. Some nineteen officers, Americans or with USA connections, were honoured that day, six of whom had died in performance of their duties for Great Britain. The posthumous awards were received by members of the deceased men's families. Priscilla received a copy of the citation[6] with the seal of the British Embassy Washington, and another copy, on embassy notepaper, of the citation of his first DFC.[7]

Later still she received the impressive scroll, decorated with the Royal Coat of Arms, 'Sent by Command of the King' which was sent to the families of all who had lost their lives in the service of their country. It reads:

This scroll commemorates

Squadron Leader H.M.Young, D.F.C.

Royal Air Force

held in honour as one who

served King and Country in

the world war of 1939-1945

and gave his life to save

mankind from tyranny. May

his sacrifice help to bring

the peace and freedom for

which he died.

Priscilla Rawson Young did not marry again. She spent most of her long life – she died in 2000 aged 91 – in Boston where she worked in support of local orchestras, a classical music radio station and her favourite charities, which she was able to help financially. She also spent much time at Ravenscroft, especially when her parents were getting old, and is buried nearby in the Skiff Mountain churchyard.

Priscilla took over Melvin's role as godparent to Bridget

Nendick. She sent food parcels during the war, as did Melvin's mother Fannie, and visited her in England several times after the war, when she also made journeys to Melvin's grave in Holland, at least once with his father Henry. On the first occasion in 1948, accompanied by her mother Clementine Rawson, she brought Bridget a dress which was very welcome at a time when clothing was still rationed. These visits continued for many years until Bridget was, herself, married with children. Bridget has fond memories of Priscilla, who clearly would have liked to have had children herself had it been possible. Alberta Gearing, 'Aunt Bert', also adopted Bridget as her godchild, having her to stay during holidays and leaving her money, furniture and jewellery in her will.[8]

Although this book is not concerned with the later exploits of Melvin's famous last RAF Squadron, 617, which are well documented elsewhere, it is fitting to record that they continued to undertake specialized, precision attacks on important targets, at great hazard to the crews involved. The danger of these operations is illustrated by the heroic, low-level efforts of 617 Squadron to breach the Dortmund-Ems Canal, a major German transport artery attacked many times, in September 1943. The first attempt was frustrated by bad weather, but sadly David Maltby, one of Melvin's section of three on the Dams raid, and his crew were lost in the North Sea on the way home.[9] Shortly afterwards the squadron tried again but with heavy loss, including another alumnus of Trinity College Oxford, Flight Lieutenant Ralf Allsebrook, DSO, DFC.[10]

If Melvin had survived Operation Chastise, it is possible that, like Guy Gibson, he would have been sent to America to advertise the RAF's success; but on return his life would have still been precarious. Gibson was killed on an operation in 1944. One of Melvin's 617 'A' Flight who did have a charmed life was Geoff Rice – not only did he survive colliding with the water on Operation Chastise, but on 20 December 1943 (the day of Melvin's Westminster memorial service) he was the only survivor when his aircraft was shot down, exploding in mid-air. Rice then evaded capture for six months with the help of the

Resistance before being caught and made a prisoner of war.

There are numerous memorials on which Melvin is commemo-rated. At Trinity College Oxford the library, which was itself built as a memorial to college members who died in the First World War, has two large wall boards, one for each World War. Unusually, the number of names lost in the Second World War almost equals that of the First. On most British war memorials the First greatly exceeds the Second in numbers and this near equality is at least partly due to the heavy losses in the RAF. Melvin's name appears there under his year of matriculation, 1934. On 11 November 2005, Armistice Day sixty years after the end of the Second World War, a service of remembrance was held in the College Chapel when all the names of the fallen college members from the two wars were read out.

Melvin is also commemorated on plaques in the chapels of his two schools in the USA; Webb School in California and Kent School in Connecticut. At the latter school, as previously noted, there is also a room in the admissions building dedicated to his memory; fittingly since he clearly had a great affection for Kent. At Westminster School in London he is commemorated on a board in the great 'School' room, and also in an illuminated Book of Remembrance. The Kingston Rowing Club has his name on their War Memorial. Perhaps the most impressive memorial is that to 617 Squadron at Woodhall Spa in Lincolnshire. This is in the form of a great, breached dam and Melvin's name, by virtue of the alphabet, appears next to that of Gordon Yeo his front gunner on their final flight.

Arguably the least conventional, but best known, memorial to Melvin and all his colleagues on Operation Chastise is the 1955 feature film *The Dam Busters*. Made in black and white, thus recreating the mood of wartime newsreels, it might be described as a dramatized documentary. The screenplay was by R.C. Sherriff and was based on Paul Brickhill's book of the same title and on Guy Gibson's *Enemy Coast Ahead*. Although the producers used some artistic licence, it was a relatively accurate portrayal of the Dams raid, albeit the Upkeep weapon was still on the secret list at that time. Guy Gibson was played by Richard Todd and Melvin by Richard Leech. Due to this film,

Melvin is probably better known to history by his nickname 'Dinghy'. The film helped to make Operation Chastise, deservedly, one of the most famous raids in the history of the RAF. At the time of writing there is talk of a new film about the Dam Busters.

Notes
1. Letter to Father Chalmers from Hobart Rawson, 12 June 1943.
2. Letter to Father Chalmers from Hobart Rawson, 16 June 1943.
3. Book of Wisdom of Solomon.
4. Henry Young succeeded in transferring this money to the school later in 1944, saying that it was a small gift but a token of Melvin's great affection for the school and of the memory of the happy days he spent there.
5. A fine silver bowl, with lid, inscribed in Melvin's memory resides in Freemasons Hall.
6. *London Gazette* 18 September 1942.
7. *London Gazette* 9 May 1941.
8. Private correspondence from Mrs Bridget Corby to the author.
9. David Maltby left a young widow and a two month old son.
10. Born in 1920, he went up to Oxford in 1939 but left in 1940 to join the RAF.

Epilogue

The author hopes that the reader has been presented with enough information about Henry Melvin Young to form his or her own opinion about him and his life, and will agree that Melvin's story is worth recording for posterity. He is, however, aware that he has had longer and closer involvement with the sources for this book than the reader. Accordingly he feels that a final summary is in order.

Parents are both the physical starting point for a life and, usually, the formative influence. Their own ancestry and background play a strong part. In Melvin's case we see the convergence of two families, one British and one American, who represented on their respective sides of the Atlantic the product of nineteenth century initiative and determination. It is perhaps determination to succeed that Melvin inherited as his most notable attribute. He was a capable student but not brilliant, he made himself a successful oarsman and aircraft pilot, but by his own admission was not naturally gifted, except insofar as he was physically strong.

In Melvin's paternal grandfather, Walter William Young, we see a self-made man, who rose from humble beginnings to found his own legal practice and give his children a better education than he had had. Walter was probably a difficult man at times – certainly Melvin's father, Henry, found him so – but he saw the chance to take advantage of the growing prosperity of the Victorian middle classes and get a substantial share for his family. Henry benefited from a good education at Berkhamsted School and Trinity College, Oxford, where he enjoyed rowing and acquired a law degree, which set him up with a profession.

Melvin's mother, Fannie Forester Rowan, was from a family that could be said to embody the American dream – anyone can succeed if they try. She was the product of a family that had moved to California and prospered there when it was still in the early stage of development. She herself had the advantage of good schools and travel, albeit her parents felt that a college education was inappropriate for a lady. But she was able to express herself through sport, tennis in her case, and grew up in the sunny, can-do atmosphere of Southern California. She and Henry had enough in common to fall for each other when he was making his own way in the world – sadly their backgrounds and personalities proved to be such that each preferred in the long run to live in their home countries.

Melvin spent his formative years as a well to do English child, with comfortable houses, enough money if not rich, and a nanny to look after him and his sisters. He had a good start to his education at Amesbury School, which seems to have been both efficient and humane. Then, when he was 13, the family moved to California. He had been there before, but only for visits. Now Fannie was determined that her children should experience American values and lifestyle – we can deduce that Henry was less keen on this experiment. Melvin attended a good school, Webb, and seems to have adapted reasonably well. He was able to have a horse, and thenceforth enjoyed riding – he was flat footed and so preferred sports like riding and rowing. However, he was never really happy in California, which he described to his friend and future brother-in-law, Ed Rawson, as a desert and which, in parts, it is. He would also have associated California with the tension that was now evident between his parents, due to their different opinions on the upbringing of their children and Fannie's desire to increase the family by adoption. She came from a large family, as did Henry.

The family now came to a compromise on Melvin's education which was to prove a very happy one for him. He was sent across the American continent to attend one of the best schools in the east, Kent in Connecticut. This school had been founded by an enlightened, almost saintly, clergyman, Father Sill, who was also an Anglophile – the school suited Melvin very well. He learned to row and settled in well. Also, it brought him into contact with a local family, the Rawsons, whose son was in his class, and whose daughter Priscilla he was to marry years later. The Rawson household became a second home for Melvin.

It had long been Melvin's ambition to follow his father to Oxford, and Trinity College in particular. Now as a keen oarsman there was the added stimulus of following Henry on the river. Trinity had done well in Henry's time but never got to the 'Head of the River'. Thus it was decided that, to prepare for Oxford, Melvin should go to Westminster school in London, where rowing was a principal sport. At Westminster he made a close friend, Conrad Cherry, who really was to become a distinguished oarsman (1936 Olympics). Melvin worked hard and in due course went up to Oxford.

At this point in time, 1933 during the Great Depression, his father and sisters also moved to England, but Fannie stayed in her native California. The separation of their parents caused much distress to Melvin and his sisters. In the late 1930s Melvin showed some antagonism towards his mother whom he felt had been unfair to his father. Fortunately his feelings for his mother eased during the war years and he visited her at the time of his marriage in 1942, when his letters showed that his affection for her had returned. Nonetheless it does seem that his father, Henry, was the stronger influence on his life.

Oxford, and Trinity College in particular, was clearly an indelible influence on Melvin's life, as it has been for many others. He made various gifts to Trinity, both during his life and in his will. He was to return on numerous occasions after he graduated. His tutor, Philip Landon, was a strong character who did much for Trinity College and its undergraduate members. Landon stimulated both sporting and academic success and was a significant influence on a generation of Trinity men. He encouraged Melvin and certainly helped him to persevere as an oarsman until finally, in his fourth and postgraduate year, he got into the Oxford eight and rowed against Cambridge on the Thames. And that same year (1938) he helped Trinity to become

Head of the River, thus realizing ambitions of both his father and Philip Landon.

At Oxford Melvin displayed an affinity for military activities to the extent that he was a member of the Officers Training Corps (Cavalry) and eventually was admitted to the Oxford University Air Squadron, with which he learned to fly. He also devoted enough of his time to his studies and, in 1937, achieved a good degree in law. He intended to follow a career in the law. He registered as a student at Gray's Inn, with a view to possibly becoming a barrister; however by his own admission he felt that advocacy might not be his forte and expected to become a solicitor. Had Melvin survived the war it is probable that he would indeed have become a lawyer, possibly in Britain but equally likely in Priscilla's native New England.

After Oxford he spent that uneasy year leading up to the Second World War with rowing, more legal studies and some tutoring at Landon's request. At about this time we see the influence of two people – his friend and former teacher the Revd. A.H. 'Bill' Franklin and Father Bernard Clements, the vicar of All Saints, Margaret Street, London. Bill Franklin introduced Melvin to Freemasonry with its rituals and mutually supportive brotherhood. Father Clements, a noted orator and charismatic personality, was an Anglican priest of the high church, 'Oxford Movement' persuasion, favouring 'Catholic' rituals but stopping short of obedience to the Pope. These two influences seem to have been complementary and show a desire on Melvin's part to be part of ordered and hierarchical institutions. He gave his religion as Church of England and seems to have followed the routine observances without displaying exceptional devotion – fairly typical for his time and background.

Also at this time Melvin was blessed with the support of his devoted godmother Alberta Gearing, at whose apartment in Kensington he had a room. This would have been especially welcome since his father now lived outside London and was re-establishing himself in the law after the American interlude. Also in the years immediately before the war Melvin's connection with the Rawson family was reinforced by visits to England by Priscilla Rawson. Melvin had known Priscilla since 1930, then as the somewhat older sister of a classmate, but now as a charming and cultivated lady who was at least as well read as himself.

Then in September 1939 war began and Melvin found himself, like many others, on a path from which there was to be no return. It is interesting that it did give him a sense of purpose after an uncertain period hoping for peace, and his letters in the first year of the war showed that he was happier with his inner self. Melvin did well on his Service Flying Training course, albeit being judged more suitable as a bomber pilot than for fighters. He got on well with his fellows, though perhaps, like other university graduates such as his colleague Leonard Cheshire, was teased for being an intellectual – but not, it must be said, a long haired one, since Melvin was very conventional in his dress and appearance. He was of a generally quiet nature in company but was not above initiating arguments on obscure topics. He was known for his habit of sitting cross legged and his ability to down a pint of beer in one go.

When Melvin started his operational career his determination showed in his insistence that his crew learned all their drills thoroughly and in his own knowledge of the duties of the others in his aircraft. This stood them all in good stead when he was forced to ditch his aircraft in the sea on two occasions – good fortune aided by his disciplined approach saw them survive. He earned a well deserved DFC from his first tour of operations.

Although he did not display the obvious aggression of some famous RAF heroes (e.g. Gibson or Bader) his was more a quiet determination to do his best to bring his country to eventual victory. He worked without complaint in 1941 as an instructor between tours, although expressing a preference for the hazards of operations over those of flying training. Thus he was pleased when he was posted back to a frontline squadron. Not surprisingly, by 1942, he did express in private correspondence a forlorn hope that the war would soon be over. By that time and serving in unpleasant conditions in Egypt he was noted as being single-minded and sometimes brusque with some ground personnel, such as intelligence officers. However, in this period he showed considerable powers of leadership and organizing ability and was awarded a Bar to his DFC. He seems to have got on well generally with his colleagues and won the confidence of his superiors, notably Philip Beare in 102 and 104 Squadrons but also Guy Gibson who, although a very different personality, shared and valued Melvin's determined attitude to the job in hand.

The end of his second tour in 1942 presented him with a welcome change – a posting to the USA – and this gave him chance to show the romantic side of his character. His first action on arriving in the USA was to visit and propose marriage to his long time lady friend, Priscilla Rawson. This he did without any preliminary courtship, demonstrating that he was able to grasp an opportunity, no doubt long wished for, when the chance arose. They were married in the chapel of his old school at Kent. He took his new bride on a honeymoon to California where he seems to have been reconciled with his mother. His duties in the USA were as a liaison officer at a flying school run by the RAF in Georgia. The company of his new wife and the hospitality of his American hosts made this one of the happiest times of his life, albeit both he and Priscilla knew that he would soon return to hazardous operations.

His return to operations was indeed hazardous – Operation Chastise. Melvin had to combine getting used to a new crew (who were inexperienced), a new type of aircraft, practising low flying by day and night and considerable training and administrative duties as the senior flight commander of the squadron, all in a period of less than two months. His maturity and experience now came to the fore and he achieved all that was required of him. He had trained and disciplined his own crew well, so that when tested they were to deliver their weapon with destructive effect – all the more tragic that they were to die at the last hurdle on the flight home.

In the final analysis, we can say of Melvin Young that he was:

A strong and determined man, matured beyond his years by his efforts to achieve his ambitions and by the hardship of war,

A quiet, well read and thoughtful man who enjoyed an ordered life and the companionship of like minded people,

A constant friend and, for a few happy months, a devoted husband to his wife Priscilla,

A good man and a hero – and on this note Priscilla should have the last word, as she told her niece, 'Melvin loved flying and was proud to be in the RAF'.

Appendix

Flights from Egypt to USA, July 1942

Courtesy of ACM Sir Thomas Prickett KCB DSO DFC RAF Retired, from his logbook.

These flights were operated by Pan American World Airways, using DC3 aircraft except for the sector Fish Lake, Liberia to Natal, Brazil which was in a Clipper flying boat.

July 24	Heliopolis (Cairo) – Wadi Seidna	5:45
July 25	Wadi Seidna – El Fasher	3:15
	El Fasher – Kano (Nigeria)	7:45
July 26	Kano – Lagos	3:00
	Lagos – Accra	1:30
July 27	Accra – Roberts Field (Liberia)	4:30
	Roberts Field – Fish Lake	1:00
July 27/28	Fish Lake – Natal (Brazil)	11:20
July 28	Natal – Belem	5:10
July 29	Belem – Georgetown (British Guiana)	4:30
	Georgetown – Trinidad	3:00
	Trinidad – Puerto Rico	5:00
July 30	Puerto Rico – Miami	5:00

July 31   Miami – Washington   6:00

                 Total flying hours for 14 sectors 66:45

Bibliography

Books

Anon, *Air Bridge*, HMSO, 1945
– *Air-Sea Rescue*, HMSO, 1942
– *Pilot's and Flight Engineer's Notes for Lancaster Aircraft*, HMSO, 1944
– *Pilot's Notes for Wellington Aircraft*, HMSO, 1944
– *RAF Middle East*, HMSO, 1945
– *The Air Battle of Malta*, HMSO, 1944
Arthur, Max, *There Shall Be Wings*, Hodder & Stoughton, 1993
Boyle, Andrew, *No Passing Glory*, Collins, 1955
Brickhill, Paul, *The Dam Busters*, Pan, 1954
Chappell, F.R., *Wellington Wings*, Crecy Books, 1992
Cheshire, Leonard, *Bomber Pilot*, White Lion Publishers, 1973
Cooper, Alan W.,*The Men Who Breached the Dams*, William Kimber, 1982
Driesschen, Jan van den, *We Will Remember Them – Guy Gibson and the Dambusters*, Erskine Press, 2004
Euler, Helmuth, *The Dams Raid Through The Lens*, After the Battle, 2001
Falconer, Jonathan, *The Dam Busters*, Sutton Publishing, 2003
Flower, Stephen, *A Hell of a Bomb*, Tempus, 2002
Galloway and Rawll, *Good and Faithful Servants – All Saints' Margaret Street and its Incumbents*, Churchman Publishing Ltd, 1988
Gann, Ernest K., *Fate Is The Hunter*, Touchstone, 1986
Gibson, Guy, *Enemy Coast Ahead*, Michael Joseph, 1946
Holland, James, *Fortress Malta*, Phoenix, 2003
Hopkins, Clare, *Trinity – 450 years of an Oxford College Community*, Oxford University Press, 2005
Humphries, Harry, *Living with Heroes – The Dam Busters*, Erskine Press, 2003
Jacobs, Peter, *The Lancaster Story*, Cassell, 2002
Morris, Richard, *Guy Gibson*, Penguin, 1994
– *Cheshire*, Penguin, 2002

Ottaway, Susan, *Dambuster – A Life of Guy Gibson VC*, Pen & Sword Books, 1994

Pitchfork, Graham, *Shot Down and in the Drink*, National Archives, 2005

Ramsden, John, *The Dam Busters*, (British Film Guide), I B Tauris & Co Ltd, 2003

Rivaz, R.C., *Tail Gunner*, Isis Publishing Ltd, 1997

Stephens, Harrison, *Webb – 75 Years of Building Character*, The Webb Schools, 1997

Sutherland, Jonathan and Canwell, Diane, *The RAF Air Sea Rescue Service 1918-1986*, Pen & Sword Books, 2005

Sweetman, John, *Bomber Crew*, Abacus, 2005

– *The Dambusters Raid*, Cassell, 2002

Sweetman, John, Coward, David and Johnstone, Gary, *The Dambusters*, Time Warner, 2003

Thomson, Ian, *Tribute to Seven*, British Publishing Co. Ltd, 1947

Other Sources

Leach, Ray, *Who was Dinghy Young?*, Air Enthusiast/Forty Four, 1991

LIFE magazine, 2 December 1940 (Atlantic Crossing on US Destroyer, William L. White)

Shortland, Jim, *The Dambusters Raid – in perspective*, (Despatches, IWM, April 2003)

The Atlantic Report, December 1943

TIME magazine, 31 May 1943

Wixey, Ken, *Armstrong Whitworth Whitley*, (Warpaint Series No. 21)

Index